Proxy Warfare

Proxy Warfare

A NDREW M UMFORD

polity

First published in 2013 by Polity Press

Polity Press
65 Bridge Street
Cambridge CB2 1UR, UK

Polity Press
350 Main Street
Malden, MA 02148, USA

ISBN-13: 978-0-7456-5118-7
ISBN-13: 978-0-7456-5119-4(pb)

A catalogue record for this book is available from the British Library.

Typeset in 10.25 on 13 pt Scala
by Servis Filmsetting Ltd, Stockport, Cheshire
Printed and bound in Great Britain by Clays Ltd, St Ives plc

The publisher has used its best endeavours to ensure that the URLs for external websites referred to in this book are correct and active at the time of going to press. However, the publisher has no responsibility for the websites and can make no guarantee that a site will remain live or that the content is or will remain appropriate.

Every effort has been made to trace all copyright holders, but if any have been inadvertently overlooked the publisher will be pleased to include any necessary credits in any subsequent reprint or edition.

For further information on Polity, visit our website: www.politybooks.com

For Hannah

Contents

Acknowledgements

My first debt of gratitude must go to Louise Knight at Polity for showing faith in a sketchy idea and guiding the book skilfully along with wonderful patience and enthusiasm. David Winters has also been of valuable assistance during the whole process.

I am thankful to my colleagues within the School of Politics and International Relations at the University of Nottingham, especially those within the Centre for Conflict, Security and Terrorism, who have debated the facets of proxy war with me. The arguments in the book are sharper for their insights.

The Plymouth International Studies Centre was kind enough to give me the opportunity to deliver some of the key ideas in the book at an invitational lecture. The probing questions I faced afterwards helped hone my thinking on many issues.

A special thank you must be extended to the students in my Contemporary Warfare class of 2011/12 at Nottingham, who saw straight through my inclusion of proxy wars as a topic on the syllabus and rigorously engaged with the issues covered in this book. Their intellectual curiosity and insights challenged me to think harder about the dynamics of proxy wars in the modern world.

I am especially grateful to three students of mine for providing valuable research assistance. Will Jackson, Chris Anquist and Vladimir Rauta remained vigilant for useful articles, tracked down obscure references for me, and proved valuable sounding boards for my ideas.

Indebted as I am to all of the above people for their contributions and help, I of course remain solely responsible for any opinions or errors contained in the book.

My final thanks go to my wife, Hannah, to whom this book is dedicated. Her love and support enabled me to face the tyranny of the blank Word document as writing commenced. Her incisive comments helped me mould arguments as the project developed. Her warm encouragement pushed the book towards completion. For this, and so much more, I am forever grateful.

Introduction

The Rise of Proxy Wars

Proxy conflict represents a perennial strand in the history of warfare. The appeal of 'warfare on the cheap' has proved an irresistible strategic allure for nations through the centuries. However, proxy wars remain a missing link in contemporary war and security studies. They are historically ubiquitous yet chronically under-analysed. This book attempts to rectify this situation by assessing the dynamics and lineage of proxy warfare from the Cold War to the War on Terror, and analysing them within a conceptual framework to help us explain their appeal. The following chapters will set the international political and strategic background of proxy warfare in the modern world, tracing its development throughout the last century, and posit it as a highly pertinent factor in the character of contemporary conflict. Also addressed are questions of what defines a proxy war; why they appeal; and who fights in them. Furthermore, the book will emphasize why, given the direction of the War on Terror and the prominence now achieved by non-state actors in the Arab Spring, this is an important time to be studying the phenomenon of proxy warfare.

Proxy wars are defined here as the indirect engagement in a conflict by third parties wishing to influence its strategic outcome. As we will see, this prevents confusion with direct intervention or covert action. Theoretically, it will be argued that recourse to proxy war has been a perpetual element of modern warfare, and will continue to be so, because the attainment of a preferred strategic outcome in a certain conflict is outweighed by consequences of direct engagement based on an assessment of interest, ideology and risk. This tendency has been particularly prevalent since 1945, as the shadow of nuclear war ensured more acute selectivity in conflict engagement given the consequences of a potential nuclear exchange. Where state or group survival is not at stake but the augmentation of interest can still be achieved, states and sub-state groups have historically proven to be conspicuous users of proxy methods as a means of securing particular conflict outcomes.

The aim of this book is not to give a potted history of every proxy war fought in the modern world. Instead, it will utilize empirical examples to flesh out the concept of war by proxy and offer up explanations for their causes, conduct and consequences in the past, present and future.

Stand-alone analysis of proxy war has largely been overlooked in security studies scholarship.[1] In 1996, K. J. Holsti asserted that 'war has been the major focus of international relations studies for the past three centuries.'[2] Yet this is only strictly true if we take a meaning of war that specifically covers conventionally fought inter-state conflict. The indirect engagement in violence – of both an inter- and intra-state variety – has been distinctly peripheral in discussions on the shape of modern war. A significant portion of the theoretical, causal and quantitative studies of war in the modern world overlook conflict in its proxy form.[3] Even substantial works, such as Odd Arne Westad's *The Global Cold War*, do not substantially promulgate a conceptual understanding of proxy war despite presenting a narrative of superpower intervention in the Third World during that era.[4] Arguably, this is because such conflicts form a major part of the background fabric of Cold War historiography. As a concept, proxy war has not been an adept cross-disciplinary traveller. This book is an effort to take the large, but undiscerning, historical literature on proxy war and lever greater conceptual understanding from it for an international relations and security studies audience.

Clausewitzean strategic thought emphasizes the changing characteristics – or 'grammar' – of warfare from era to era. It is this book's goal to demonstrate how the evolving 'grammar' of warfare in the modern world has rendered shifts in the way in which proxy wars have been perceived by states and non-state actors and thus effected their utility as a mode of strategic attainment. In the twentieth century, at the dawn of the era of total war, the mode of proxy intervention took on new resonance as the consequences of engaging in outright war came with heightened risk of high death tolls, infrastructural destruction and political annihilation. The end of the Second World War ushered in the nuclear era, starkly accentuating the risks associated with going to war or challenging the security of a nuclear nation. This nuclear weapon-induced stability/instability paradox arguably caused nations to find alternative outlets for their strategic ambitions, where the consequences were contained yet the rewards tangible. The global reach of the Cold War soon demonstrated, in the mid-twentieth century, that engagement in proxy wars was a convenient means by which the superpower states could exert their influence and attempt to maximize their interests in parts of the Third World, while simultaneously reducing the risk of conflict escalation.

Even after the bipolar system gave way to the New World Order in the 1990s, proxy intervention continued to be a recurrent element in international conflict, as a new age of globalization gave rise to the information revolution and bore witness to the increased prominence of the non-state actor in international relations. During the last decade of the twentieth century, the notion of 'intervention' became explicitly tied to the nascent 'responsibility to protect' agenda and the debates surrounding humanitarianism.[5] This, to a large

extent, overshadowed the continued presence of proxy interventions undertaken for reasons entirely alien to the liberal
foreign policy agenda of that decade in the West.

The appeal of proxy war is undiminished in the post-9/11
world whereby states 'with or against' the United States, in
President George W. Bush's dichotomization of world politics, jostled to secure their own strategic interests as the War
on Terror came to dominate the discourse of international
relations in the early twenty-first century. As state sponsors
of terrorism coalesced to form Bush's self-proclaimed 'axis
of evil', the mode by which both the 'coalition of the willing'
and the constituents of the axis (and, significantly, their allies)
could further their strategic aims has manifest itself in large
part through the wider employment of proxies.

Yet it is not just superpowers that have shaped the terrain
of proxy warfare. Given its lower-cost, often lower-risk, mode
of conflict engagement, non-state actors including terrorist
groups and more recently private security companies have
been utilized as proxies. This book will therefore explore the
wide spectrum of actors involved in proxy warfare, historically
and contemporaneously, in order to fully analyse not only
those states who sponsor proxies in conflicts, but also assess
the motivations of those groups who act as the proxies themselves.

So why is proxy war an important issue in the modern
world? It is largely because of two major trends in the analysis
of war. First, in the words of John Mueller, is the 'obsolescence of major war'.[6] Total warfare, or conventional 'state
versus state' conflicts between developed countries, is a form
of conflict that has diminished given the changing nature of
the system of statehood and the international order in the
mid-to-late twentieth century. Second, history tells us that
any rigorous academic and military focus upon counter-
insurgency (as currently witnessed during the War on Terror)

is momentary and often lasts only as long as the deployment of troops. The scholarly output surrounding the Vietnam War is prodigious, yet reflections upon the nature and mode of counter-insurgency waned once the US withdrew. As a consequence, the American military (and indeed its academic community) has had to 'relearn' counter-insurgency since the degeneration of the wars in Afghanistan and Iraq into asymmetric conflict quagmires. Yet, if the pattern of attention granted irregular warfare after the Vietnam pull-out is repeated after combat troops have departed the frontline of the War on Terror, then this will inevitably relegate counter-insurgency once more to the strategic backburner.[7] So when combined with the fading of traditional state-based conflict and the searing effect of the Iraq and Afghanistan wars on prospective American willingness to deploy troops in large numbers again to fight asymmetric opponents, the future direction of warfare could be heavily influenced by an increased reliance on proxy conflict.

The book will be broken down into analytically focused chapters that seek to deconstruct the essential elements that constitute wars by proxy. Each chapter will provide in-depth case studies to help put some empirical meat on the conceptual bones of the analysis. Chapter 1 will deconstruct *what* proxy war actually is. It will establish the contours of this particular form of conflict, locating it in the wider picture of modern warfare. This chapter will elaborate upon the definition offered earlier that proxy warfare is the indirect engagement in a conflict by third parties wishing to influence its strategic outcome. Often subsumed into the wider narrative of the history of warfare, this chapter will argue for the need to view this specific strand of war in isolation, constitutive as it is of particular motives, practices and component players. The reader will be encouraged to observe the ubiquity of proxy war in modern conflict history. The question of what proxy war is will be illuminated by highlighting specifically what it is not. Proxy war does not include the overt supply of troops. This constitutes direct third-party intervention, and this delineation will be offered in this chapter in order to adequately define the phenomenon of proxy war itself.

Chapter 2 will address the fundamental question of *why* proxy intervention appeals to actors in international relations. Based on assessments of self-interest, it will be argued that recourse to proxy involvement is often a way of realizing long-term strategic foreign and security policy goals, either regionally or globally. Proxy intervention crosses the state/sub-state divide given its proclivity towards furthering strategic goals regardless of unit status, hence the engagement by non-state actors in proxy war also. Although, it must be noted, historically superpowers have preserved a higher propensity for proxy intervention. This chapter will identify the primary reasons, based on assumptions of self-interest, as to why proxy interventions occur, namely, ideological interventions motivated by grand political desires (especially during the Cold War) and interventions prompted by security or strategic designs.

Chapter 3 asks '*who* engages in proxy war?' It will identify the sources of state-based intervention, but will also unpack assumptions as to the monopoly that states have upon engaging in proxy warfare by accounting for the role that non-state actors can play, such as terrorist groups and militia organizations. This chapter will assess the sources of proxy intervention in conflicts, highlighting prevalent cases of state engagement in proxy war (such as initial American involvement in the Vietnam War), as well as sources of non-state involvement, ranging from terrorist groups (such as Hezbollah's role during the Israeli war with Lebanon in 2006), and ethnic diasporas (such as Irish-Americans during the Northern Irish 'Troubles').

Chapter 4 tackles the question of *how* proxy wars are fought. It will critically assess the forms of support proxies receive from third parties, such as intelligence assistance, money and logistical provision. This chapter tracks the forms of intervention by which states and non-state actors engage in proxy war. It will disaggregate these modes of involvement into three main categories. The provision or training of manpower, such as co-opted militias or other irregular combatants, has often been the most prevalent way of engaging in proxy war in order for third parties to ensure direct leverage on the existing conflict. The supply of material and money is often a popular recourse to covert involvement by proxy, allowing third parties to act as distant benefactors to their preferred warring faction. Finally, the sharing or dissemination of information is a means of subtly influencing events, for example, by spreading propaganda or utilizing the Internet as a mode of sharing information that would undermine an opponent.

Chapter 5 turns its attention to the *future* of proxy war, analysing trends in warfare and conceptualizing proxy war as a foreseeably prevalent component of conflict as the twenty-first century unfolds. Superpowers, particularly the United States, have historically harnessed proxy intervention as a mode of achieving a political endgame. American presidents of both parties have not been prepared to forfeit US interests, yet often, as Vietnam demonstrated, and Iraq may yet prove, certain watershed events create the conditions whereby future strategic interests are no longer willing or able to be secured by expensive and comprehensive displays of American military prowess. The so-called 'Vietnam Syndrome' saw a nation emerge from a protracted and costly conflict in South East Asia, cowed by its humbling at the hands of a supposedly ill-trained and ill-equipped insurgent force. It would not be until the Gulf War of 1990/91 that the American's deployed their troops in anything like such numbers again. So if the

Americans are unwilling to sacrifice their interests abroad, yet are reluctant to pay the price for doing so, how can it resolve this conundrum? This book posits that the inevitable consequence of the War on Terror on the American purse (with the Iraq War alone estimated to eventually cost $3trillion in the midst of a global financial downturn[8]) and on American national pride (with over 4,000 combat deaths even after President Bush proclaimed 'mission accomplished' in May 2003) is that the US will revert to engagement in proxy warfare, to maximize their interests while minimizing their political and military exposure. In short, the signposts of post-Iraq conflict in the world point towards the re-emergence of proxy warfare as a primary mode of intervention, violence and (dis)order.

Yet proxy war is not an American-centric phenomenon. The continuing rise of China as a global superpower raises significant questions as to how it will exert its presence internationally and whether this actually increases the likelihood of it engaging in proxy wars without damaging its trade relations with the West. Ongoing civil wars in Africa have provided a forum for China to exert its power regionally and may represent the beginning of a more assertive Chinese foreign policy in the coming decades.

It must be added that proxy war is not a form of conflict conducted solely by states. It is very important to address the issue of what proxy warfare means in the age of non-state actors and networked terrorism. The establishment of global al-Qaeda 'franchises' has distinctly affected the mode by which regional conflicts can be influenced by the proxy involvement of such networked cells, particularly at the behest or with the cooperation of 'rogue states'. Furthermore, the rise to prevalence in the late 1990s of private military corporations arguably represents another significant signpost for the future direction of proxy warfare, representing a new high-profile vehicle for the undertaking of proxy intervention. Even after the eventual American withdrawal from Afghanistan, the US will certainly still wish to exert influence over the security situation in that country and the wider region. The harnessing of proxy actors to do their bidding for them becomes an inevitable consequence, and as such will represent a large plank of the discussion in this forward-looking chapter.

The conclusion will reiterate the way in which proxy warfare has been a perennial element of modern warfare, and is deserving of sustained analysis and critical reflection. Crucially, it will also holistically assess, from the vantage point of history, the outcomes of proxy wars by identifying common determinants of success and failure across the empirical examples highlighted in the chapters. This will help conceive of the whole gamut of dynamics impinging upon proxy wars and enable a thorough deconstruction of the consequences proxy wars have had, not only upon the countries in which they have been waged, but on the landscape of modern warfare as well. In other words, is proxy intervention historically proven to be a viable means of achieving goals and augmenting interest, and if so what can the past tell us about the future direction of proxy war-fighting?

Proxy intervention has been prevalent across the entire spectrum of warfare in the contemporary era, from conventional state-versus-state wars, to the multiplicity of civil wars across continents; from the pockets of insurgencies that now dominate strategic discourse, to the undeclared or limited wars that offer the opportunity of simmering tensions to disguise proxy interference. The conclusion will seek to establish the assessment of proxy war as an identifiable strand of future war studies, particularly given the indications that it is a mode of warfare that we are likely to see more, and not less of, in the coming decades. Proxy wars cut across and between the multiple layers of global security (international, regional, state and sub-state), and as a result a thorough understanding of the issues, threats and conduct of proxy wars upon these different levels will help us think about how to assess the future direction of this integral element of modern conflict.

CHAPTER ONE

What is Proxy War?

Proxy wars are the indirect engagement in a conflict by third parties wishing to influence its strategic outcome. They are constitutive of a relationship between a benefactor, who is a state or non-state actor external to the dynamic of an existing conflict, and their chosen proxies who are the conduit for weapons, training and funding from the benefactor. Such arm's-length interventions are undertaken ostensibly for reasons of maximizing interest, while at the same time minimizing risk. In short, proxy wars are the logical replacement for states seeking to further their own strategic goals yet at the same time avoid engaging in direct, costly and bloody warfare.[1]

Before we go any further, it is important to place proxy wars in both their international and local context. Often, the two contexts work in partnership to shape the dynamic of the conflict. Historically, states have exploited specific localized events (such as a civil war) to engender a shift in the wider geopolitical environment (such as the stifling of a rival ideology in the broader region). Take, for example, the Thirty Years War (1618–48), where Protestant France and Catholic Spain covertly involved themselves on the sides of their co-religionists within the Holy Roman Empire. Two centuries later, the American Civil War can be seen through the prism of proxy warfare, whereby British weapons sales to the Confederacy was widely interpreted as London attempting to lever long-term political and economic gain from the victory of the secessionist Southern states.[2] Likewise, during the Franco–Prussian War of 1870–71, Britain again vicariously influenced events by arming the French military to undermine their common Prussian enemy. Even before the nineteenth century had ended, the Industrial Revolution's impact upon the weapons of war had increased the scope for Western nations in particular to stake claims in foreign conflicts. The production of more deadly and efficient weapons became bargaining tools for strategic influence over the outcomes of wars.[3]

Although proxies have been utilized throughout history as means of fulfilling the objectives of third parties, it was only in the twentieth century that war by proxy was transformed into a prolific form of conflict. Despite an official position of neutrality, the United States, through massive arms supplies, used the Triple Entente as a proxy to shape events in Europe from a distance during the opening three years of the First World War. President Franklin D. Roosevelt adopted a similar stance of proxy engagement during the Second World War up to 1941.

Indeed, the adoption of proxy war strategies became so ingrained into the politics of the mid-twentieth century that direct superpower intervention (such as the Soviet Union's invasion of Afghanistan) arguably became the exception rather than the rule of conflict during the Cold War period. Proxy interference from a distance had established itself as the norm. Assertions, such as that from Harold Tillema, that in the late Cold War era 'foreign overt military intervention directs modern international armed conflict',[4] are blind to the prevalence of foreign covert and indirect military intervention and the ubiquity of proxy wars throughout that century.

Defining the Parameters of Proxy Wars

Although efforts have been made in the past to explain what proxy wars entail, certain areas of definitional contention still remain. In 1964, Karl Deutsch termed proxy wars 'an international conflict between two foreign powers, fought out on the soil of a third country; disguised as a conflict over an internal issue of that country; and using some of that country's manpower, resources and territory as a means for achieving preponderantly foreign goals and foreign strategies'.[5] Arguably, though, Deutsch's definition is too state-centric, as it ignores the role non-state actors can play in proxy wars (as discussed here in chapter 3), and it unnecessarily internationalizes proxy wars (an inevitability, perhaps, of the Cold War context in which this definition was coined) by overlooking the often regional power struggles that they represent.

So perhaps in order to garner a greater understanding of what proxy wars are, it would be useful to first dwell upon what they are not. Proxy wars are not merely regional wars that seemingly mirror broader ideological struggles perpetrated by superpowers. Neither are they exercises in direct military intervention by third parties or necessarily a form of 'covert action', as shall be discussed more fully later in this chapter. Proxy wars need not be solely categorized as occurring when, for example, medium regional powers clashed during the Cold War, as such an assumption ignores other forms of conflict in which proxy interventions occur, namely, civil wars.

A further effort at clarification is needed because in this book the terms 'proxy war' and 'proxy intervention' will be used interchangeably. This is based on an understanding that states primarily intervene indirectly in the wars of others, using proxies who are already engaged in the war. The conditions of war already exist and are often exacerbated by the intervention. Furthermore, these indirect interventions are used to enhance inherently war-like strategies of interest or ideology maximization, albeit ones that minimize the risks associated with outright war or direct intervention. As such, this book will refer to proxy wars and proxy interventions to explain the same phenomenon of indirect interference in an existing conflict by a third-party state.

Richard Ned Lebow, in his book *Why Nations Fight*, characterized Cold War confrontations between the two main superpowers and the allies of their opponents (understood in this book as a proxy war if the ally receives indirect forms of aid from the other superpower) as an 'in-between state', neither war nor peace, and therefore not included in his large dataset analysis of the causality of wars over the last three centuries.[6] This is symptomatic of how an understanding of the dynamics and importance of proxy wars has fallen through the cracks of security studies and contributed to incomplete scholarship of the full spectrum of war typologies in the modern world. This is a significant omission, especially when considering K. J. Holsti's calculation that 30 per cent of all wars between 1945 and 1995 witnessed some form of external intervention[7] – although we can assume that this figure is actually much higher given that Holsti did not include in his dataset the wars of decolonization that occurred across the Third World in the mid--twentieth century, many of which contained demonstrable proxy interference from superpower benefactors. Indeed, it was the patterns of proxy intervention in such anti-colonial wars that denoted an increased prevalence of proxy war, as superpowers sought ways to shift regional politics in their ideological favour. As Hedley Bull noted in the early 1980s: 'In recent decades . . . modes of intervention have changed . . . [F]orcible intervention has tended to give place to non-forcible, direct to indirect, and open to clandestine.'[8]

Until now, one of the most substantial efforts to recognize proxy war as a strand of conflict worth studying in its own right lay in an article written in the mid-1980s by Israeli scholar Yaacov Bar-Siman-Tov.[9] In this article, he poses nine key questions in order to characterize 'war by proxy as a separate and unique category of war'.[10] It is worth addressing each of these questions in turn and offering some answers, so as to flesh out our understanding of what proxy war constitutes:

- *Can one classify as a proxy war one in which an external power intervenes directly?*
  No. *Indirect* intervention is the fundamental element of proxy war (see the later section for a full discussion of this issue).
- *Is it essential that both small states in a local war serve as a proxy for an external power?*
  No. The premise that proxy wars build upon inter-state conflicts is misleading; however, it is not indicative of such wars to be symmetrical in their provision of proxies. Furthermore, such wars are not confined to 'small states' acting as the proxy (as the final question addresses), as this assumes that proxy wars only grow out of pre-existing inter-state wars between such states. They can feed off other forms of war too, and involve large states or non-state actors.
- *Can we regard a war by proxy for one side and not the other?*
  Yes. Take, for example, the Soviet occupation of Afghanistan between 1979 and 1989. For the Soviets, this war consti- tuted a direct intervention involving the overt deployment of large numbers of their own troops in order to prop up an allied regime. For the Americans, however, it presented itself as an opportunity to engage in a proxy war by funding and arming the *mujahedeen* fighters who wished to repel the Soviets. The same war therefore represented two distinct forms of intervention, one direct and one by proxy, for the two main superpowers (see the next section on the dynam- ics of proxy wars for a further discussion of this issue).
- *Does the consideration of the war by one external party as a war by proxy make it possible to define a war as such, or do we need more external parties to define it as a war by proxy?*

No. The categorization of a conflict as a proxy war is not necessarily for states themselves to certify. Indeed, external parties are more likely to refer to it as 'foreign internal assistance', 'long-range projection capabilities', or some other such semantic device.

- *Does the consideration of the war by the external parties as a war by proxy make it possible to define a war as such, or do we need it to be considered as a proxy war by one or both of the small states?*

No. Again, it is less the involved parties who are likely to classify themselves as being engaged in a proxy war, but more likely the wider, non-involved, international community. But the more important point remains not who asked whom to intervene (for example, a client-state request or a benefactor-state offer), but how the very presence of externally provided arms or money is affecting the dynamic of that war.

- *How does one distinguish between proxy relationships and alliance relationships?*

On occasion, with difficulty. It is often pre-existing alliances between states that lead to the request for, or offer of, proxy intervention. However, it remains important for us to distinguish between the meaning of an ally as a treaty-bound friend willing to share in the blood cost of a war to achieve a shared strategic vision, and a benefactor state utilizing a proxy war strategy exactly because they are not willing to share that burden. A proxy relationship is therefore far more impermanent, temperamental and opportunistic than alliance relationships, which are often built on more common foundations of shared identity or threat perceptions.

- *When is a big state helping a small state and when is it using the latter?*

This comes down to a subjective interpretation of the motive behind the intervention (see chapter 2 for a thorough discussion of these motives). We always need to bear in mind what Bertil Dunér has labelled the 'compatibility of interests' during such interventions.[11] This is the foundation of the benefactor–proxy relationship, as it reveals the perceived mutual benefit that the intervention reaps if the strategic goal motivating the proxy war is achieved. This, however, must be couched in terms of the asymmetry between the actors, traditionally (but not exclusively) encompassing a more powerful resource-rich state and a less influential state or non-state proxy.

- *Does a big state act as a proxy for a small state?*
On occasion, yes. This answer in large part is predicated upon an understanding that big states can unwittingly fight a proxy war on a smaller state's behalf. The American-led invasion of Iraq in 2003 and the toppling of Saddam Hussein's regime, for example, fulfilled a long-term Iranian ambition by cementing Tehran as a pre-eminent regional power despite the American's lack of desire for this outcome. The fulfilment of a strategic goal by proxy does not necessarily have to be a conscious or deliberate act.
- *Is the definition of the term 'war by proxy' limited only to big power–small state relationships?*
No. Proxy wars are not fought exclusively by or for states. Particularly in the post-Cold War period, non-state actors have been harnessed as proxies (such as the utilization of Hamas by Syria to attack Israel). Chapter 3 engages in detail with exactly who fights proxy wars, and explores the dynamic between states and non-state actors.

The Dynamics of Proxy Wars

The relationship between benefactors and their proxies are context specific and are mired in a host of queries relating to consent, levels of engagement, and the perception of eventual gain.[12] If we take the use of proxy wars by the Soviet Union during the 1970s as an example, we can see, as Bruce Porter has pointed out, that in the vast majority of cases 'the initial impetus for Soviet military assistance . . . was a specific request from the Third World client, rather than an offer from Moscow'.[13] This has implications for our understanding of the phenomenon of proxy wars, as it indicates that they are not inherently the product of overbearing interference from larger external powers, but often invited opportunities to achieve a mutual strategic goal. The outcomes, regardless of the initial cause or motive, are, however, still invariably the same: the ratcheting up of regional tensions and the flooding of the country with arms, money or foreign 'advisers'.

The issue of pre-existing alliances between eventual benefactors and clients, of course, can play a large role in the explanation of a proxy wars occurrence. If alliance reliability affects whether nations decide to go to war in a conventional inter-state conflict (such as the treaty entanglements that spiralled into the First World War), then there is no reason to assume that the level of support from allies has to first be restricted to war in an inter-state sense, second be direct, and third be overt. Complex conflict dynamics, or the desire to avoid sparking international opprobrium, may provoke certain alliances to manifest their solidarity in a proxy manner. If, as Alastair Smith has argued, a nation is more likely to retaliate if provoked when it expects the support of its allies,[14] then we must consider that the fulfilment of collective security pacts and alliance treaties can be achieved both through direct third-party intervention and by indirect proxy involvement.

Yet one of the most concerning dynamics of proxy wars remains the way in which they possess the capacity to potentially escalate localized conflict into larger wars. The issue of escalation has to be disaggregated between the potential for indirect proxy assistance to cause more deaths within a civil war, for example, because of the proliferation of weapons, even though the initial conflict remains contained within its original borders; and its potential to escalate a conflict beyond its original borders by triggering collective security pacts amongst neighbouring states or drawing in another major power. The historical record of proxy wars has shown a detrimental proclivity towards the first type of escalation, yet a relative absence of the second. Morton Halperin argued in 1963 that what he called 'local wars' (essentially contained regional conflicts with superpower proxy interference) did not escalate into 'central wars' (a wider, potentially nuclear, war between the superpowers) because of the interplay between four main factors: the foreign policy objectives of each side (which often revolved around minimizing involvement in costly foreign wars); the estimated risk of conflict escalation (in particular, the desire to avoid nuclear tensions); respective images of the role of force (namely, a mutual understanding of the seeming utility of proxy intervention); and domestic political objectives (specifically, the public ramifications of the heightened potential for all-out war). When combined, Halperin argued, these factors created a mutual US-Soviet appreciation of the dangers of conflict escalation. These criteria ensured that proxy wars in the early Cold War period – and arguably throughout that era – remained contained conflicts that did not provoke overt international crises between Washington and Moscow.[15]

As an intermediate position between non-intervention and direct intervention, another key dynamic of proxy wars to consider is their fluid nature, both in terms of the relationship between the benefactor and the proxy, and then in terms of the size and scope of the intervention itself. Benefactor–proxy relations can fluctuate over time. On occasions, the affiliation deteriorates and the proxy no longer serves a strategic function for the benefactor, either because the strategic dynamic of the whole conflict has evolved, or because the military performance of the proxy is insufficient, too risky or below par. Yet, on other occasions, that leverage of the proxy grows and a power shift occurs in the relationship with the benefactor state. Stemming from such a shift can be the emergence of a far more equitable alliance between the two, with the proxy able to define more of its own political objectives and military strategy independently. This, for example, occurred in respect to the relationship between Syria and Hizballah after 2005 (see chapter 3 for a full exploration of this case).

In terms of the second fluid dynamic of such conflicts, we can establish that the size and scope of proxy wars do not necessarily remain static. They can develop into outright interventions, as the American involvement in Vietnam during the early 1960s demonstrated. During John F. Kennedy's presidency, the number of US military 'advisers' in Vietnam had risen from 685 to 16,732.[16] This was to be a proxy war on a grand scale whose strategy, Stanley Karnow has argued, was based on Kennedy's opposition to 'the introduction of American combat troops in Vietnam, though he had no intention of accepting defeat'.[17] The large incremental increase in American 'foreign internal assistance' in Vietnam snowballed to such an extent that the original strategic parameters that cautioned against direct intervention were cast aside by President Lyndon Johnson after the aggrandized incident in the Gulf of Tonkin in August 1964. Therefore, we can see how in this example an initial small-scale proxy war developed into a large-scale proxy war, and then morphed into a massive ground war. The Vietnam War is important empirical proof of how we must differentiate proxy intervention (initially with non-combatant military 'advisers') from the eventual direct intervention that followed (which caused the deaths of approximately 56,000 American soldiers). It is worth exploring this difference in more detail.

How Proxy Intervention Differs from Direct Intervention and Covert Action

In the late 1960s, Hans Morgenthau noted how direct third-party interventions 'serving national power interests' had been an 'ancient and well-established instrument of foreign policy'.[18] However, it is the purpose of this book to demonstrate the long-standing proclivity that states, and indeed non-state actors, have had for *in*direct interventions by proxy. In order to achieve this, it is necessary to sketch out exactly how indirect intervention by proxy is worthy of separate conceptual boundaries from those drawn for direct methods of intervention, including covert action.

Patrick Regan defines intervention as: 'convention-breaking military and/or economic activities in the internal affairs of a foreign country targeted at the authority structures of the government with the aim of affecting the balance of power'.[19] Yet this definition retains an inbuilt assumption that all external interventions are state-instigated (as only states are bound by conventions) and overt. Such assumptions help explain the low visibility of discussions in the literature about the often covert proxy interventions that have occurred in recent decades. Further assumptions as to the purpose of intervention being predicated upon inherent desires to bring stability to a specific country or region (as Regan posits too[20]) also drastically overlook the thoroughly unaltruistic mode in which many interventions are taken in order to bring about *in*stability (to the cost of a rival regional power, for example).

Any definition of proxy war that includes direct military intervention misinterprets what should arguably be seen as the fundamental cornerstone of our understanding of proxy war: *indirect* interference. Direct interference constitutes a third-party intervention and represents a different mode of conflict as a state, for example, becomes willing to pay a blood price for achieving a strategic objective by putting its own troops in harm's way. A proxy war strategy, on the other hand, circumvents this age-old moral risk of war. There is, however, one caveat. Third-party interventions can constitute a mode of proxy war if conducted by a surrogate force on behalf of a non-intervening conduit. The most notable Cold War-era example of such a situation occurred at the outbreak of the Angolan Civil War in 1975, when Cuban troops staged a direct inter-vention but under the auspices of a Soviet proxy war against pro-American forces. Thus, in such cases, the benefactor remains indirectly involved (the USSR supplied weapons and funding) and lets a third party surrogate force stage an armed intervention on its behalf (Cuba provided the manpower). Yet this distinction becomes nullified if the benefactor starts to intervene directly itself, cancelling out the need for proxies.

A more contemporary illustration of this crucial distinction between direct and indirect forms of intervention has arisen with the heated debate about the increasing use of robotics and technology in warfare. The proliferation of unmanned aerial vehicles (UAVs) in the war in Afghanistan – particu-larly their use by the US military and Central Intelligence Agency (CIA) in the Federally Administered Tribal Areas of Pakistan – has brought the use of drones to the heart of the American campaign to eradicate terrorist leaders.[21] Indeed, the then Director of the CIA, Leon Panetta, went as far as to call drone strikes 'the only game in town in terms of trying to disrupt the Al-Qaeda leadership'.[22] This assessment was consolidated in 2012, when *The New York Times* revealed that President Obama personally oversees a terrorist 'kill list', reserving for himself the final authorization of a drone strike on targeted operatives.[23] Members of Obama's national security team talked of the president's approval of 'lethal action without hand-wringing', while critics of his reliance on drones argued that UAV attacks only provide a short-term tactical fix and deviate the White House from seeking long-term strategic solutions to Islamist terrorism.[24] Such criticisms, however, have not deterred US military and CIA efforts to bring UAVs to the heart of their counter-terrorism efforts. Their appeal lies in their lightweight, human-free manoeuvrability. They are also comparatively cheaper and more durable than a regular military plane. A Predator drone (one of the most commonly used UAVs) costs $4.5million, which is eighty-five times less than an F-22 fighter jet, and it can be airborne for up to twenty-four hours at a time.[25] Consequently, drones have a financial and human cost appeal to governments. If a Predator is shot down, there are no concerns over the loss of a pilot's life (this, of course, assumes a disregard of the high possibility of innocent civilian 'collateral damage'). Instead, drones operating over Afghanistan and Pakistan today are piloted over 7,000 miles away from a US Air Force base in Nevada. They use satellite communications to control the drone's take-off, landing and missile release (usually a laser-guided Hellfire missile). Although initially only used for surveillance purposes, the Predators were soon weaponized, allowing for precision strike coordination from a very long distance. By 2008, the US had over 5,000 drones at its disposal – double the number of aircraft manned by human pilots.[26]

Yet the absence of a human pilot does not mean that we should automatically assume that drones are new proxies in the sky. The removal of military personnel from the aerial vehicle is of itself not a fundamental reason to categorize drone attacks as a facet of proxy war. The exclusively technological component of this form of warfare does not render drones a mechanism of assassination by proxy. The drones may be indirectly piloted but they are fulfilling a substantive *direct* military function. Drones carry US military markings, sometimes including the American flag. Although made of composite materials and controlled by satellite, drones are another manifestation of how a state directly wages war on another state or non-state actor. Drone warfare may be innovative, even futuristic, in its conceptualization, but it remains as direct a form of warfare as a manned aerial bombardment or a missile attack launched from a warship. The only way in which drones could be used in a proxy war context would be if they were being used covertly on behalf of another state or group in a conflict in which the US was playing no direct part. But their utilization at the moment by the US to further their war effort by direct methods in Afghanistan means the drone is not presently a tool of proxy war. That is not, however, to discount its potential use in such conflicts in the future.

It is the fundamental distinction between direct and indirect forms of intervention that result in the need to disaggregate proxy wars from the broader term 'covert action'. The CIA formally defines covert action as: 'An operation designed to influence governments, events, organizations, or persons in a manner that is not necessarily attributable to the sponsoring power; it may include political, economic, propaganda or paramilitary activities'.[27] On the surface of it, such a definition shares many commonalities with the characteristics of proxy wars, including their often clandestine nature, the utilization of numerous tactics and the goal of influencing outcomes. Yet beneath the veneer, covert and proxy wars are differentiated by key issues that necessitate separate categorization.[28] Fundamentally, covert action requires a state to place intelligence or special forces operatives inside another country. This represents a form of *direct* intervention. The covert nature of such actions does not nullify the fact that State A has placed agents inside State B in order to conduct what William 'Wild Bill' Donovan, legendary head of the wartime American

Office of Strategic Services (OSS), tellingly labelled 'subversive operations abroad'.[29] Proxy wars may also be conducted covertly but they rest on an underlying premise of *indirect* direct engagement, with State A hiring proxies in State B to conduct 'subversive operations' for them. Intelligence agencies and special forces personnel, of course, play roles in the prosecution of proxy wars, but this is only in a training and advisory capacity. Furthermore, it should also be noted that just like other direct forms of intervention, covert action can be a next step taken by states once a proxy war strategy has been initiated. Proxy wars can morph into more direct forms of covert action.[30]

On a similar theme, the dual employment of a proxy war strategy alongside a direct interventionist strategy also need not be seen as contradictory. The efforts in 2011 to overthrow Libyan leader Colonel Muammer Gaddafi are an ideal illustration of how they are not mutually exclusive. Keen to usher in a new political order in Libya, but reluctant to fully commit military resources to make this happen, certain NATO countries undertook an aggressive air campaign to directly assist rebel forces by bombing Gaddafi's military compounds and communication hubs. This overt use of force became the most visual representation of interventionist regime change. However, a parallel proxy war strategy was also undertaken by external powers in order to undermine Gaddafi and boost the rebel cause indirectly too. Leaked documents suggest that in March 2011, towards the beginning of the uprising, the Americans requested that their Saudi Arabian allies supply weapons to the anti-Gaddafi rebels by proxy, although it remains to be seen whether this request was enacted.[31] As the uprising gathered momentum during the spring of that year, levels of American and British proxy involvement increased, with decisions taken by both countries to provide telecommunications equipment to the rebels in order to improve their ability to coordinate attacks on Gaddafi's forces.[32] By June, the multinational Contact Group on Libya met in Abu Dhabi and collectively pledged a donation of over $1 billion to the political wing of the rebel movement, the National Transitional Council (NTC). This financial act of proxy intervention was hoped to augment rebel potency so they could purchase their own weapons.[33] NATO air strikes may have grabbed the headlines in relation to the eventual overthrow of Colonel Gaddafi, but proxy interference helped ease the rebels to victory via indirect support mechanisms.

The Spanish Civil War (1936–9) is another prime example of how direct and indirect interventions can coexist in the same battlespace. In this case, we can see how external support for two internecine warring factions can constitute a direct third-party intervention (that of Nazi Germany in support of General Francisco Franco's Nationalists) and a proxy war (that of the Comintern's arm's-length creation of the International Brigades) at the same time. The proxy war characterization of a conflict need not apply to all involved parties, as this particular case study will demonstrate.

Case Study: The Spanish Civil War

It has been a common intellectual trend to perceive the high levels of intervention in the Spanish Civil War as a foretaste of the wider struggle between fascism and its opponents that would engulf the rest of Europe in 1939.[34] Antony Beevor has gone as far as to label the Spanish Civil War a 'world war by proxy' given how the quantity of external intervention was indicative of the fomenting ideological struggles that the wider continent was experiencing.[35] Yet we should deepen our interpretation of the events in Spain during this conflict in order to see how they represented an opportunity for fascist Germany and Italy, and the communist Soviet Union, to retard the spread of their rivals' ideology without the official declaration of war. The strategic interest in the outcome of the Spanish Civil War was important for the repercussions it would entail not so much inside Spain, but beyond its borders. To this extent, the Spanish Civil War draws fewer analogies with the Second World War and more with the later ideological battles of the Cold War, whereby exogenous interference in intra-state conflicts became a standardized practice of proxy superpower involvement.[36]

Even though both warring factions in Spain were in receipt of significant amounts of aid, weapons and funding from external sources, the crucial difference remained the German and Italian provision of combat personnel, sanctioned by Hitler and Mussolini, for the nationalist cause of General Francisco Franco. This stood in contrast to the republican's reliance on foreign volunteers to augment their fighting force and the non-intervention pact adhered to by the Allied powers (minus the political and logistical guidance offered by the Soviet Union). This indirect Soviet involvement was coordinated in a devolved manner by the Comintern and not centrally through the Kremlin, thus fostering an even greater proxy war prism through which to view this conflict.

In August 1936, in the wake of Franco's coup, the Comintern sent delegates to Spain, while Stalin authorized the first Soviet arms shipment to aid their Spanish comrades. This Soviet aid, however, was not altruistically donated to the republican cause. The Russians took large payments from the republican government's share of the Spanish gold reserve as payment for supplies.[37] It was arguably the receipt of this Soviet aid that enabled the Spanish Communist Party to dominate the spectrum of anti-fascist factions, in large part due to the sheer quantity of materiel received. Within a month of Stalin's orders, the USSR had transported around 100 aircraft and 100 tanks, along with a plethora of guns, ammunition, transport trucks and armoured vehicles to Spain.[38] Import–export firms were established in cities across Europe, each controlled by a representative of the Soviet secret police, the NKVD, as a front for arms trafficking to Spain.[39] Declassified Russian documents reveal that between October 1936 and August 1938, the USSR sent fifty-two ships laden with weapons bound for Spain. Included in these shipments were an accumulative 331 tanks, 657 aircraft, and over 400,000 guns.[40]

Yet these arms shipments were not the most significant contingent of the communist proxy war in Spain. In September 1936, the Comintern decided to create the International Brigades as a mass volunteer surrogate force to aid the republican war effort. Throughout the war, 32–35,000 men of fifty-three different nationalities signed up to serve in its ranks.[41] This number is a testament to the Comintern's policy of requiring each Communist Party in both Eastern and Western Europe to raise a requisite number of recruits.[42] Yet despite their multinational composition, the International Brigades were unquestionably Soviet in their leadership. Interpretations of the Brigades as Soviet surrogates are reinforced by the consistent presence of at least 800 Soviet military 'advisers' throughout the war, who oversaw the training and command of Brigade units.

Within the first four months of the war it had become evident that a major proxy war effort on behalf of the Soviet Union, both through indirect weapons provision and the vicarious supply of surrogate forces via the Comintern, was having a demonstrable impact upon the shape of the conflict. This was most apparent when assessing the vital role that the International Brigades played in preventing the fall of Madrid to Franco's forces as early as November 1936.[43] So concerned were the fascist allies of Franco as to the discernible advantage that indirect Soviet assistance was granting the republicans that Germany in particular sought to increase their involvement in Spain in a more direct manner. The creation and deployment of the infamous Condor Legion in November 1936 was to prove the most overt sign of direct German interference in Spain. The Legion constituted around 100 aircraft (whose most notorious involvement in the war came when they carpet-bombed the Basque town of Guernica on 26 April 1937), 24 tanks and approximately 5,000 military personnel.[44] By early 1937, these German numbers were complemented by the arrival of 17,000 Italians (predominantly soldiers), deployed on the orders of Mussolini. These Axis power direct troop deployments were thought to roughly mirror the numbers of communist surrogate proxies in the International Brigades who had crossed into Spain by the end of 1936.[45]

The Spanish Civil War acts as a stark reminder of how two warring parties can use mutually reinforcing propaganda to ratchet up levels of external intervention of either a direct or indirect nature. Both the republicans and nationalists played upon fears of malign fascist and communist interference respectively, in order to encourage international allies to send help in the spirit of solidarity. The forthcoming nature of external support as seeming vindication of the rivals' propaganda helped escalate the war and provided for differing sorts of intervention to occur at the same time: a direct fascist intervention through troop deployment, and a proxy communist intervention through the utilization of surrogate forces and weapons supply.

Building upon this understanding of the ways in which proxy wars can be located within other forms of conflict, the next chapter deconstructs the reasons why proxy wars are fought and helps explain why they are so appealing to those who engage in them.

CHAPTER TWO

Why Does Proxy War Appeal?

Proxy wars occur when states or non-state actors, based on a perception of interest, ideology and risk accept that direct intervention in a conflict would be either unjustifiable, too costly (politically, financially or materially), avoidable, illegitimate or unfeasible. This chapter aims to explore how states come to these assumptions by ascertaining why proxy wars appeal to those who become involved in them. What characteristics do proxy wars possess that encourage participants? How can we theoretically conceptualize the motives that states and non-state actors have for undertaking acts of indirect intervention in the wars of others? And why are proxy interventions undertaken and favoured over other modes of intervention?

Theorizing Proxy Wars

This book is premised upon a multitheoretical understanding as to why proxy wars appeal. At its heart there is an accepted realist assumption that calculations made by states and non-state actors whether or not to intervene by proxy are predicated upon an inescapable acknowledgement of self-interest. This chapter will offer up empirical examples that highlight this fundamental motive as a reason for seeking minimal input but maximum gain out of foreign wars. Although this may be the foundation, realism is a useful but not wholly adequate theoretical tool. Given the complexities of proxy wars, any theoretical explanation of the phenomenon must reflect such intricacies by broadening the horizons of our understanding and acknowledging the relevance of certain tenets from alternative theoretical schools. So, for example, this chapter holds that liberal notions of the 'obsolescence of major war' have a lot to tell us about the appeal indirect intervention holds. Furthermore, it is argued that realism does not account sufficiently for the important role ideological motives play in the adoption of proxy war strategies because of the integral part ideology has in identity formation and thus alliance construction. It also contends that an engagement with perceptions of risk is also vital to garnering a more holistic understanding of the allure of 'plausible deniability' in a proxy war setting.

Back in the mid-1970s, Frederic Pearson identified six primary reasons why states intervene in other countries.[1] Although he did not explicitly refer to proxy intervention, it is clear that the criteria he laid out certainly cover some of the essential motives behind indirect intervention explored in this book:

1. Territorial acquisition (*via the expansion of a regional 'sphere of influence' in a proxy war sense*).
2. Protection of social groups (*hence the inclusion of issues relating to identity formation and the role ethnic diasporas can play in proxy wars in this book*).
3. Protection of economic interests (*such as, for example, proxy wars undertaken to garner control of resources, as discussion of Chinese proxy war strategies in Africa will show in chapter 5*).
4. Protection of diplomatic or military interests.
5. Ideology.
6. Regional power balances.

In addition to Pearson's list, several more motives need to be added if we are to perceive the full gamut of reasons why proxy wars are undertaken.

7. Perception of probable success (*mainly in relation to the detriment caused to a rival directly involved in the conflict*).
8. Perception of conflict escalation (*nominally the avoidance of it, as could occur if a direct intervention was undertaken*).

Taken together, the rest of the chapter will explore how these various motives have come to shape the way in which proxy wars have been so prevalent in international relations, and allow us to further understand why indirect intervention appeals. This is based on a belief that the reliance on one single theoretical school blinkers our ability to see the interconnectedness of these motives. As the historical record demonstrates, numerous catalysts sit side by side when analysing the causes of proxy wars. To briefly return to the case study in the previous chapter, we can see that the Soviet Union launched a proxy war in Spain for two main reasons: to halt the spread of fascism, and to ensure that the domestic politics of the Spanish republican movement would come under Soviet control.[2] This dual explanation displays parallel motivations for proxy war initiation: ideology *and* interest.

Interest, Power and Proxy Wars

As a catalyst for war, interest has been a perpetual element of realpolitik explanations of conflict. It has been taken as the cornerstone of state motivations and is seen as the primary causal factor in creating clashes between states. By way of illustration, K. J. Holsti has argued that war can be characterized as 'a rational if not always desirable activity, a means to a known end defined in terms of state or national interests'.[3] Although referring exclusively to modes of conventional inter-state war, this assessment is worth deconstructing through the lens of proxy wars because of the ways in which expressions of mutual interest motivate benefactors and clients in proxy war scenarios. During the Cold War, to take perhaps the most obvious example, the two main superpowers expended much interest in the Third World in order, as Steven David has argued, to fulfil 'the traditional desire of a great power to extend its influence beyond its borders'.[4]

It is arguable, however, that both the benefactor and proxy have divergent as well as mutual interests vested in the outcome of a conflict. Although the initial intervention is often predicated upon an expression of interest by the benefactor, the proxy also retains an interest in maintaining the relationship due to the developing levels of dependency for material support, the potential success in the war they are engaged in, and the acknowledged mutual desire to defeat a common enemy.[5]

The most vivid illustration of this mutual dependency based on divergent interests is the American adoption of a proxy war strategy at the beginning of the Second World War. In the years of European crisis in the run up to the outbreak of the war, the US Congress passed a series of Neutrality Acts that proscribed loans, the provision of weaponry or material assistance to any nation at war in the world. However, upon the commencement of hostilities in 1939, President Franklin D. Roosevelt pressured Congress to permit the sale of arms to the Allied powers. The German blitzkrieg of 1940 softened the entrenched isolationism of American congressional opinion, resulting in the approval of a 500 per cent increase in defence spending at the behest of an openly interventionist Roosevelt.[6] The first major act of American proxy intervention came with the president's 1940 decision to trade Britain fifty US Navy destroyers in return for ninety-nine-year leases on eight strategically important military bases.[7] But the most significant act of war by proxy against the fascist states of the European Axis came with the passing of the Lend-Lease Bill in March 1941. It allowed Roosevelt to circumvent the restrictions of the

Neutrality Acts by not selling but lending or leasing Britain military equipment to the eventual tune of $30 billion.[8] David Reynolds has argued that the Roosevelt administration came to see that 'large-scale material support for Britain was the best way to keep the war away from America and give the US time to rearm'.[9] In other words, it was a proxy war of self-preservation, designed to serve the interests of the homeland well above the interests of her allies. Mark Stoler concurs, arguing that the calculus of interest upon which Roosevelt's proxy war strategy was built means that we must interpret American actions as being 'not motivated by altruism. Rather it was based on a clear recognition that Germany constituted a threat to them as well as to Britain, that Britain's continued survival in the war and victory over Germany were therefore in American interest.'[10]

Yet there is reason to believe that such overtly interest-motivated actions are the exception rather than the norm. In a large dataset study of the causes of ninety-four major wars from 1648 to 2008, Richard Ned Lebow argued that security or material interest sparked only twenty-seven of these conflicts.[11] Interest is therefore only part of the story, whether looking at major inter-state war, as Lebow was, or proxy wars as we are here. Other significant aspects must be factored into the equation if we are to ascertain a holistic understanding of why proxy wars appeal. Foremost amongst these are ideological motives.

Ideological Motives for Proxy Wars

In his seminal post-Cold War book, *We Now Know*, John Lewis Gaddis argued that the corpus of work produced on relations between the US and the USSR before its collapse had been inadequate. Access to the partially opened archives in the former Soviet Union had revealed to historians,

Gaddis argued, how much scholars had underestimated the importance of ideology in the decision-making process, and how interest was interpreted through ideological lenses.[12] Although the role of ideology may have been overlooked, it certainly did not go unnoticed. As Neil MacFarlane noted in the mid-1980s: 'to exclude entirely the possibility that ideology influences behaviour . . . is to maintain that there is no relation between belief and action and between strategy and policy'.[13] An analysis of Soviet foreign and security policy during the Cold War years reveals an ideologically informed rationale that was used as a precursor to proxy intervention. Celeste Wallander argued that Soviet actions in the Third World rested on an assessment of three key variables: 'the escalatory link between local and general war; the nature of socialist internationalist duty to aid progressive change; and the likelihood and sources of national liberation and the development of socialism'.[14] Soviet thinking in relation to the necessity of exporting their ideology developed over time. Stalin's rejection of Lenin's legacy of promoting worldwide revolution in favour of enhancing communism 'in one country' ensured a relative level of Soviet introspection, until Nikita Khrushchev's enunciation of a strategy of support for wars of 'national liberation' in the Third World, in the early 1960s. This newly imbued sense of internationalism was predicated upon the notion that global politics was the manifestation of a mass class struggle between the forces of capitalism and communism, with Moscow dutybound to aid the exponents of communism. Yet the Kremlin would only pick communist proxies engaged in wars of 'national liberation' if they were on an 'acceptable' path to communism. The Soviet's certainly expected a *quid pro quo* from these proxies. Aid, arms and ammunition were only delivered in return for ideological subservience.[15] But, importantly, Moscow would only select pro-communist allies that were in power. The Soviets tended to avoid sponsoring non-state groups, such as terrorist organizations. Such a conservative attitude towards violent sub-state action in large part was due to latent concerns about the risks of conflict escalation and the negligible chances of potential success.[16]

When interpreting the role that ideology plays in perceptions of proxy war's appeal, we therefore must layer it on top of the pervasive role that interest plays, as discussed in the previous section. The two are arguably entwined. Even the doyen of classical realism, Hans Morgenthau, felt compelled to characterize superpower proxy intervention in the Cold War as 'ideological shadow-boxing' that was motivated by 'respective national interests'.[17] Such ideologically informed, interest-based policymaking shines through when analysing key moments from Cold War history. Take, for example, how in June 1961, in the wake of unfruitful discussions with Khrushchev at the Vienna Summit over the Berlin crisis, President John F. Kennedy sought ways to reassert American interests and reinforce the strength of global democracy. He alluded to how greater proxy intervention in Vietnam could be utilized as a means to achieve this: 'Now we have a problem in making our power credible and Vietnam is the place.'[18] This manifestation of ideologically driven interest maximization was reinforced by the way in which the foreign policy officials who shaped the Kennedy administration's agenda were the combat generation of the Second World War. As Frank Costigliola points out, these policymakers 'imprinted with what they regarded as the lesson of Munich . . . concluded that 'totalitarian' states, including the Soviet Union and the People's Republic of China, were expansionist and ideological. As a consequence, the democracies had to remain armed, vigilant and opposed to "appeasement".'[19] In the early 1980s, Michael Doyle argued that: 'US Cold War policy cannot be explained without reference to US liberalism. Liberalism creates both the hostility to communism, not just to Soviet power, and the crusading ideological bent of policy.'[20]

Yet the ending of the Cold War did not also terminate American predilection for foreign policies of a 'crusading ideological bent'. The neo-conservatives who came to dominate the administration of George W. Bush brought about 'a revolution in American foreign policy' in line with their ideologically infused world view.[21] This 'revolution' was premised on an aggressive unilateralism that prioritized preemption over containment, regime change over negotiation, and informal coalitions over institution-bound alliances. Neo-conservatism 'purposefully place[d] the United States on a war-footing' as the Bush administration sought interventionist ways to expand their brand of liberal democracy across the Middle East after the 9/11 attacks, as a way of protecting themselves from future threats.[22]

As examples utilized throughout this book will argue, American proxy interventions both during and indeed after the Cold War have been undertaken to fulfil President Woodrow Wilson's value-laden objective of 'making the world safe for democracy'. This understanding of why proxy wars appeal, in this example to the US, tells us how such a world power views itself and its role in the world; how it has attempted to project its ideology and identity on to others; and how all of this impacts upon global order. In short, ideological norms and ideals have an explanatory value alongside interest and power when assessing the appeal of proxy wars.

Such a worldview clearly legitimized the use of proxy war as a mechanism to achieve such goals, as demonstrated by the State Department asserting to President Kennedy the necessity of preventing the further expansion of communism in South East Asia. Kennedy acknowledged the benefits of a war by proxy in Vietnam when he noted 'the reluctance of the American people and of many distinguished military leaders to see any direct involvement of US troops in that part of the world'.[23] Secretary of Defence Robert McNamara aired his concerns regarding 'the uncertainties of our ability to deal with it [Vietnam] by military means', and began pushing for efforts to augment the South Vietnamese government's capability to fight the war itself – in essence, to commit the US to an outright proxy war strategy.[24] President Kennedy seemed to accept this argument and warded off advice to introduce combat troops, preferring instead in November 1961 to again increase the number of military advisers to assist in implementing the Strategic Hamlets programme, designed to relocate entire villages perceived to be vulnerable to Viet Cong subversion. In short, as Odd Arne Westad has argued, both 'the United States and the Soviet Union were driven to intervene in the Third World by the ideologies inherent in their politics'.[25]

Yet it is not just 'irregular' wars against insurgent enemies that have come to mould our understanding of why proxy wars occur. The adoption of an arm's-length strategy of intervention is the result not only of an interest-based desire to shore-up an ideological ally, but is also the product of shifts in the very nature of warfare itself.

The 'Obsolescence of Major War'

The avoidance of nuclear war has been a prime reason for the enhancement of proxy war strategies.[26] The Cold War tendency for superpowers to provide weapons and military 'advisers' to their preferred clients in the Third World only exacerbated this trend. Thus, prolific American and Soviet indirect engagement in foreign conflicts ensured that proxy wars acted as a loosening of the valve on the pressure cooker that was Cold War geopolitics. The Cold War remained 'cold' for a reason: the emergence of nuclear weapons had ensured that 'hot' wars between superpowers would have such unparalleled consequences as to make direct conflict between the two morally unthinkable.

Resting on a Kantian liberal notion that war is an abhorrent institution, a key work to influence the debate surrounding the nature of contemporary conflict was John Mueller's book *Retreat from Doomsday*. In this book, Mueller argued that major war in the modern world could be unlearned by humans, citing how 'once popular, even once-admirable institutions in the developed world have been, or are being eliminated because at some point they begin to seem repulsive, immoral and uncivilized'.[27] Mueller utilizes the examples of slavery and duelling to demonstrate how it is possible for major war between developed nations to be added to this category of outdated activities.

Yet despite more and more states opting out of what Mueller calls 'the war system', as the twentieth century matured, this does not necessarily mean that pacifism triumphed. Instead states, mainly superpowers, which were still observant of their interests or ideological positioning, have pursued alternative avenues for attaining strategic advantage. One such avenue is the pursuit of weapons sales by states to partners in a proxy effort to secure the interests of themselves and their allies. Let us label it 'arm's-length arms dealing'. Between 2003 and 2006, international arms transfer agreements were reached with a total value of $160 billion. Developing nations were involved in two thirds of all these agreements.[28] During this period, the US ranked as the world's most prolific weapons supplier, delivering a third of the total. Russia came second, providing a quarter of all weapons sold.[29] From this, we can infer that although the Cold War is over in name, US–Russian competition for influence and interest in the developing world is still rife.

Weapons sales demonstrate one key way in which states can

militarily bolster an ally by proxy, whether that ally is at war or not. They represent another example of how states engage in indirect intervention in foreign conflicts or crucibles of simmering regional tensions via the provision of military hardware. One of the starkest examples of weapon sales as a proxy war strategy is that of American arms deliveries to Israel. Since 1976, Israel has been America's largest aid recipient. For the thirty years since assistance began, the aid has averaged out at over $2 billion per year. Significantly, around two thirds of this money has been earmarked for military support.[30] Israeli efforts to produce new weapons systems, such as the Lavi aircraft, have been boosted by the Americans to the tune of $3 billion. This is on top of the delivery of US Blackhawk helicopters and F-16 jets.[31] All US military equipment sold to Israel is done so on the proviso that it is used for 'internal security or defensive purposes' only.[32] Yet on several occasions the US has noted Israel's contravention of these regulations. In 1982, the Reagan administration suspended sales of cluster bombs to Israel after reports that the Israeli Defence Force (IDF) had used such US-made weapons during the invasion of Lebanon that year. Furthermore, in 2001, Congressional investigations took place to uncover whether Israel had used American Apache helicopters to kill key Palestinian leaders.[33] All of this military hardware was provided to Israel despite the US not being directly involved in any of the wars Israel has fought with its Arab neighbours, or in its internal counter-terrorism efforts. Yet, as John Mearsheimer and Stephen Walt observe, 'it is hard to think of another instance where one country has provided another with a similar level of material and diplomatic support for such an extended period'.[34] This is arguably because it can be seen as the most palpable example of a *preventive* proxy war strategy at work. The US is ensuring, by proxy, that neighbouring states are deterred from invading Israel or engaging it in conventional battle. America is indirectly guaranteeing Israeli security by using arms sales as a means of indirectly influencing the security situation in the Middle East and cementing the perceived mutual interests of the two nations.

Major war may well be archaic, but the mode by which interests are pursued or ideologies spread have changed accordingly. Slavery and duelling may have fallen by the wayside as Mueller observed, but that is not to say that alternative forms of human exploitation or violent forms of dispute settlement did not emerge in their place. Traditional inter-state conflict may have declined since the Second World War, yet the number of civil wars, for example, increased as the twentieth century drew to a close. This magnified the scope for interested states to remain detached from such internecine conflict yet still secure favourable outcomes through co-opted proxies. Simply put, the obsolescence of major war has come at the price of the emergence of widespread proxy war, including preventive proxy wars, as the US-Israel weapons deals infer. One of the primary reasons for this rise is the differentiation in risk perception that proxy war holds in comparison to major war.

Risk and Proxy War

In his seminal book, *War in an Age of Risk*, Christopher Coker argues that war has fundamentally 'become risk management in all but name'.[35] Proxy war typifies this assertion. The risks associated with direct intervention in inter- or intra-state wars are self-evident: international condemnation; loss of life to military personnel; high financial costs of lengthy and substantial deployments; and the potential embarrassment of open strategic failure. Proxy intervention circumvents these risks to a large, but by no means total, degree. As Coker goes on to argue, 'the language and method of risk analysis is also applied not only to the way we conceive war but also the way in which we conduct it'.[36] Logically, such an understanding helps us envisage the appeal of waging indirect – and often covert – wars, in order to lever as much gain out of the wars of others without having to assume the burden of the risks listed above that are associated with conventional warfare.

One of the major elements of risk that proxy wars avoid is the potential for conflict escalation. If, as Charles Gochman and Russell Leng have argued, 'the demonstration of power in the context of militarized inter-state disputes involves the willingness to risk escalation for the purpose of showing resolve',[37] then the demonstration of power in the context of proxy intervention involves the willingness to defuse escalation for the purpose of masking resolve. Take, for example, the way in which the then President of Pakistan, Zia ul-Haq, became conscious of the inherent risks relating to conflict escalation that a brazen proxy war strategy could bring to the Soviet occupation of neighbouring Afghanistan in 1979. Ul-Haq allowed Pakistan to become the main conduit for American weapons to be passed on to the Afghan mujahedeen who were resisting the Soviets (for a full case study, see chapter 4). In discussions with the CIA Director William Casey, ul-Haq told Casey that the US should only supply the mujahedeen with enough weapons to 'keep the pot boiling' because large-scale weapons supply may cause the 'pot to boil over' and risked Soviet retaliation on Pakistan.[38]

Such examples of escalation awareness are to a great extent explained by the way in which proxy wars offer the cloak of 'plausible deniability' to those engaging in them. By avoiding the risks associated with direct intervention, as listed above, proxy war-wagers are opting into a scenario whereby their indirect, perhaps covert, mode of conflict intervention creates an opportunity to mask the scope of their involvement and avoid potential recriminations. The ways in which proxy wars are fought (as fully discussed in chapter 4) allow for a more discrete influence to be exercised over a foreign war. The credence of the 'plausible deniability' arguments rests on the absence of foreign-state soldiers with 'boots on the ground' in a war zone, or any other visible signs of direct interference. Plausible deniability therefore becomes an integral part of how the proxy war can be seen as an archetypal exercise in risk management.

Although recourse to proxy intervention fulfils realist prescriptions for furthering self-interest, the integral desire to avoid overspill into overt or more total forms of war ensures that our understanding of risk has to dilute more concentrated realist perceptions of interest maximization as attainable at any cost. By way of illustration, Bruce Porter has argued that there is evidence to suggest that the adoption of a proxy war strategy by the Soviet Union in the 1970s was undertaken with a large degree of restraint. For example, Porter points to how the Kremlin did not sell long-range bombers or missiles capable of striking major enemy population centres during their interventions in the Ogaden War in Ethiopia and Yom Kippur War in Israel.[39] This restraint reinforces the fundamental appeal of war by proxy, namely, the avoidance of large-scale deployments that would provide wider hostility or incur a militarized response in kind by other actors.

Restraint and risk are integral parts of an understanding of how the concept of the 'security dilemma' can be applied to an analysis of war. Robert Jervis defined the 'security dilemma' as 'the means by which a state tries to increase its security [and] decrease the security of others'.[40] To a significant extent, this is what drives states to undertake proxy interventions. Alliance politics and delicate regional power balances often mean that any gains made by states (such as successfully helping overthrow an allied government of a major rival state through the indirect arming of an insurgency) can inevitably be perceived as a threat by rival states. As Jervis goes on to argue, 'decision makers act in terms of the vulnerability they feel', based firstly 'on the price they are willing to gain increments of security', and secondly on 'the perception of threat'.[41] Functionally, this means that the 'security dilemma' operates in the realm of risk management. Minimizing vulnerability to risk is a perpetual element of decision- making, particularly in the planning and execution of proxy wars. Indeed, proxy wars possess the capacity to both perpetuate and circumvent the 'security dilemma'. They can perpetuate it by demonstrating a state's resolve to achieve interest maximization or ideological consolidation beyond their borders through the evident willingness to co-opt a third party to ensure their security is increased. Conversely, proxy wars can circumvent the 'security dilemma' by resorting to covert means of intervention that attempt to invisibly increase security without evidently provoking insecurity within other states. Dilemmas prompted by the offsetting of risk against security are common to the machinations of defence and security policy, and their centrality to understandings of how proxy wars are waged should be no exception. Building upon this understanding, the next chapter explores exactly who engages in proxy war and how they seek to assert indirect interference in the wars of others.

CHAPTER THREE

Who Engages in Proxy War?

This book holds that proxy wars are constitutive of a relationship between a benefactor, who is a state or non-state actor external to the dynamic of an existing conflict, and their chosen proxies who are the conduit for weapons, training and funding from the benefactor. Therefore, the question of *who* engages in proxy wars involves a detailed look at the mechanisms of indirect assistance that are built between two or more states, between states and non-state actors, and between groups of non-state actors. Arguably, there are four identifiable types of relations between these actors that have shaped the dynamics of proxy wars in the past and present. These are when:

- a state uses another state (as a surrogate force);
- a state uses a non-state actor (such as a terrorist organization, militia group or private military company);
- a non-state actor uses a state;
- a non-state actor uses another non-state actor (as a surrogate force).

This chapter is dedicated to deconstructing these relationships and exploring how recent examples of indirect interventions reveal a broad spectrum of proxy war-wagers. It will begin by exploring how states, particularly superpowers, have come to adopt proxy war strategies as a mainstay of their interest and ideological projection capabilities. But before that discussion begins, it is worth explaining why some actors in the international system should not be classified as proxy war-wagers. Two groups in particular come to mind: non-governmental organizations (NGOs) and international organizations (IOs). Both of these actors arguably do not conform to standards constitutive of *who* fights in a proxy war because their aims and objectives do not fall within the wider boundaries of *what* constitutes a proxy war. NGOs, mainly humanitarian aid organizations, and IOs, namely the United Nations and its ad hoc peacekeeping missions, are fundamentally dedicated to the alleviation of suffering within war-torn communities and to bringing about swift and peaceful resolutions to ongoing violence. Their goals are not to bring about the victory of one side over another. Simply, their presence in a war zone does not meet the threshold of what a proxy intervention inherently is: the benefactor must want to further a *war* aim. Humanitarian aid delivery does not constitute the furtherance of a war aim; neither do multilateral efforts to keep warring factions apart. As such, it is not appropriate to classify NGOs or IOs as actors who fight proxy wars. This has mainly been the preserve of states and violent non-state actors (VNSAs).

The State and Proxy Wars

The very concept of proxy war itself, although historically ubiquitous, became indelibly associated with the machinations of Cold War superpower politics in the mid-twentieth century. It was during this period that proxy wars became a frequently used vehicle by strong states for achieving strategic goals within, and beyond, their self-styled 'spheres of influence'. The statist foundation of proxy wars was manifest by the way in which well-defined ideological principles came to encapsulate the *raison d'état* of the two superpowers of the Cold War era, and thus help shape the dynamics of the wider world order. Take by way of example the 'foreign internal assistance' programme devised by the Kennedy administration in the early 1960s, which was driven, in William Rosenau's words, by a desire to 'expand the presence of the state and to shield fragile institutions from communist subversion'.[1]

Superpower states took it as their ideological and interest-bound duty to intervene in the internal affairs of other states in order to protect them from the influence of rival powers. Indeed, this compelling urge to undertake this perceived duty became enshrined in doctrine. We saw in the last chapter how Nikita Khrushchev's promise to back 'wars of national liberation' committed the Soviet Union to a proxy war strategy in Africa and Asia. Conversely, we must also look at how the adoption of National Security Council Report #68 (commonly known as NSC-68) by President Harry Truman in April 1950 ensured that American foreign and defence policy now rested upon the assumption that, as John Lewis Gaddis has put it, 'no part of the world was now peripheral [and] that no means of protecting them could now be ruled out'.[2] NSC-68, and the so-called 'Truman Doctrine' that it spawned, therefore increased the inclination of American policymakers to perceive proxy intervention in distant conflicts as intrinsic to protecting vital national interests. As the temperature of Cold War geopolitics fluctuated, the very process of engendering a peaceable detente between the US and the USSR in the mid-1970s rested, in Janice Gross Stein's words, upon their willingness to ensure 'a reduction in the intensity and scope of involvement in proxy wars'.[3] Such interventions were thus central to the very shape of international relations itself during this period.

It is largely incontrovertible to assert that during the Cold War it was the United States and the Soviet Union who retained the most capacity for regular interventions (given both their huge defence budgets and acute sense of ideological obligation to intervene), mainly using other states or non-state actors in the Third World as their chosen proxies to prop up or unsettle other states or groups. John Lewis Gaddis again has weighed in on this issue by suggesting that modes of intervention, including those by proxy, undertaken by the two superpowers in the Third World, 'were problematic because none of these measures could prevent future defections, whether as the result of revolutions, coups, dissatisfaction, neglect or simply the other side's offer of a higher price. The Third World, then, was both victim and manipulator of the "first" and "second".'[4] Despite rightly acknowledging the impermanence of proxy war solutions, Gaddis underestimates the way in which superpower states were exploiting Third World states as agents of conflict. Proxy wars are wars of choice, not necessity. Yet the obligations that the bipolar nature of world politics placed upon the superpowers during the Cold War ensured that even localized civil wars were seen through the lens of pan-national ideological struggle. Such conflicts gave rise to superpowers exercising their patronage on warring factions, which often resulted in the utilization of a 'surrogate' force to undertake a direct intervention on their behalf. These surrogates would become the focus of condemnation, would take the responsibility for paying the blood price for achieving the strategic goal, but crucially would take orders from their benefactor. The most prominent example of this first type of proxy relationship between a state benefactor and another state proxy is the Soviet utilization of a Cuban surrogate force to intervene in the Angolan Civil War in the 1970s.

Case Study: Cuban Surrogates and the Angolan Civil War

This most bloody of African civil wars, which lasted from Angola's independence from Portugal in 1974 until a peace deal signed only in 2002, provided a tragic footnote to Cold War superpower proxy intervention in the Third World that cost the lives of half a million people.

Three main groups vied for the control of postcolonial Angola and each attracted external support as a means of achieving their goals. The Popular Movement for the Liberation of Angola (MPLA) received significant backing from the Soviet Union and Castro's regime in Cuba, as well as from like-minded socialist parties in Europe. The Front for the National Liberation of Angola (FNLA) was backed by neighbouring Zaire and had been receiving money from the US Central Intelligence Agency (CIA) for a number of years prior to decolonization. Finally, the National Union for the Total Independence of Angola (UNITA) was a breakaway group of the FNLA whose strident anti-Western agenda was aided by allies in China.[5]

Once the Portuguese withdrawal had been fully undertaken by late 1974, the three major factions began scrambling for power. Holden Roberto's FNLA received a massive rise in covert CIA funding, a move that was mirrored by the Soviets in favour of Agostinho Neto's MPLA. Emboldened by superior numbers (the FNLA containing around 10–20,000 fighters compared to the MPLAs 6–8,000) and a $300,000 donation in January 1975 from the 40 Committee (an American government secret intelligence unit that sponsored covert operations), the FNLA stepped up attacks on rival factions in an effort to cement power.[6] Not wishing to be outflanked in a proxy war, the Soviet Union responded by expanding the amount of arms it was distributing to the MPLA. The first Soviet arms shipments arrived in Angola shortly after the visit to the country by the chair of the Soviet Committee on Afro-Asian Solidarity in February 1975. Between April and June of that year the port of Luanda had received arms deliveries from at least twelve Soviet, East German, Yugoslav and Bulgarian flagged ships. In April 1975 alone, around 100,000 tonnes of arms were airlifted into Angola by the Soviets in an effort to bolster the MPLA war effort.[7]

The following month was an important one for the dynamic of this particular proxy war. In May 1975, Fidel Castro deployed the first batch of Cuban military advisers to Angola. Totalling 230, these advisers were to work alongside the MRLA – a task that Neto had requested from Moscow but that had been flatly declined. What emerged here was a clear demonstration from the Kremlin that their Angolan proxy war strategy would be compromised by any more visible signs of intervention. Yet the Soviets retained a desire to maximize their influence over the conflict in line with a perceived strategic interest; hence the permission for the MRLA to utilize Cuban advisers who could then be directed from Moscow as a surrogate force. Throughout 1975, the number of Cuban advisers proliferated in Angola to such an extent that by January 1976 there was a force of approximately 12,000.[8]

Capitalizing upon this proxy assistance, the MPLA made the most of its manpower advantage over the FNLA, who had received no advisers, but instead accepted CIA-sourced money to the tune of $32 million and weaponry worth $16 million.[9] By early 1976, the MPLA had made significant gains in the civil war to such an extent that by March that year they were in control of sufficient amounts of the country to declare themselves the government of a new People's Republic of Angola. The Soviet's proxy war strategy had seemingly paid off. When asked why the Americans were backing the FNLA, CIA Director William Colby replied in realpolitik terms: 'Because the Soviets are backing the MPLA is the simplest answer.'[10] Such an understanding reveals just how the adoption of proxy war strategies can create flash points, which in this context affected the wider geopolitics of the Cold War. Henry Kissinger himself was compelled to admit at the time that the process of detente between the superpowers could not 'survive any more Angolas'.[11] Proxy wars were draining the superpowers' resolve for maintaining cooperative relations.

Yet an understanding of proxy wars need not rest on a Waltzean conception of great power politics. Granted, superpowers have certainly utilized the strategy of war by proxy, but smaller powers have also attempted to indirectly intervene in conflicts outside their own borders. An explanation of who engages in proxy wars does not ultimately correlate with a state's power status in the broader scheme of international relations. This, in large part, is arguably down to the fact that to wage a proxy war a state does not need a sizeable military or a formidable arsenal of high-tech weaponry. It is a strategy that need not be reliant upon economic or political grandeur – merely a sense of interest or ideological maximization, achievable through ostensibly deniable and lower-cost means when compared to waging an outright intervention. It is smaller states' engagement in proxy wars that has revealed a predominant trend towards the second form of relationship mentioned at the beginning of this chapter, namely the sponsorship of a non-state actor to act as their chosen proxy. The proxy war waged by Iran during the recent American-led occupation of Iraq articulates this point clearly.

Case Study: Iranian Proxy War in Iraq since 2003

Iranian influence over politics in Iraq long pre-dates the 2003 American-led effort to topple Saddam Hussein. During the bloody and protracted Iran–Iraq War (1980–88) distinct links were forged between the government in Tehran and the Supreme Council for the Islamic Revolution in Iraq (SCIRI), a Shia group who fought on behalf of the Iranians against Saddam's regime. SCIRI, and its armed wing the

Badr Brigade, remained crucial allies of the Iranians after the launching of Operation Iraqi Freedom in March 2003. Tehran immediately began to build links inside Iraq to ensure that, by proxy, Iran could simultaneously posit itself as a key player in the rebuilding of Iraq by enhancing the strength of key Shia allies, while also, in Doran Zimmermann's words, 'calibrating disorder' within its rival neighbour in order to 'make itself an indispensable interlocutor in post-war Iraq'.[12] This dual-track strategy manifested itself through the Iranians encouraging Shia political parties, including SCIRI, to actively participate in new democratic elections, at the same time as they were nurturing Shia militia groups to intensify their insurgency against Sunni opponents and the coalition forces.

The incremental increases in Iran's proxy war efforts in Iraq are noticeable. By 2004, Tehran had located units of its clandestine paramilitary group, the Qods Force, and units of its intelligence service VEVAK, inside Iraq.[13] By mid-2006, circumstantial evidence had engendered a widespread belief amongst British military commanders in the predominantly Shia southern city of Basra that 'specialist weaponry and IED technology was being smuggled into the region from Iran'.[14] As a consequence, border security became an integral part of British security provision – crucial considering that the two British-controlled provinces of Basra and Maysan shared over 300 miles of border with Iran. Suspicions were heightened in December 2006 when US forces arrested two senior Qods Force officers at a meeting with a known Badr Brigade leader.[15] In February 2007, the Bush administration published an intelligence report which went even further than previous assessments by citing Iranian complicity 'at the highest levels' in supplying Shia militias across Iraq with IEDs, perpetuating Anglo-American diplomatic concerns at Iranian attempts to politically permeate Iraq and attain regional dominance.[16] By mid-2007, US diplomats in Iraq were so assured of Iranian influence over insurgent violence in southern Iraq that one official bluntly stated that: 'Iran is fighting a proxy war in Iraq ... They are already committing daily acts of violence against US and British forces ... The attacks are directed by the Revolutionary Guard who are connected right to the top [of the Iranian government].'[17] Even the then commander of US forces in Iraq, General David Petraeus, went out of his way to publicly accuse the Iranians of training, arming and advising militias so that they could 'fight a proxy war against the Iraqi state and coalition forces'.[18] This was informed by intelligence showing that during the US 'surge' in Iraq in 2007, which was commanded by Petraeus, the leader of the influential Mahdi Army militia group, the prominent cleric Muqtada al-Sadr, had sought sanctuary in Iran at various points in order to avoid arrest.[19]

However, it is not just arms and sanctuary that the Iranians stand accused of providing in order to encourage Shia violence in southern Iraq, but other logistical means through which they could perpetuate an insurgency by proxy. A Washington Institute for Near East Policy report concluded that Iranian support 'often arrived in the form of commodities – money, hashish, and prescription medications – that could be used to recruit young, poor foot soldiers'.[20] Conscious of the potency of outside support upon the efficacy of the British campaign in southern Iraq, even Tony Blair felt compelled to admit to the Iraq War (Chilcot) Inquiry that: 'It was the introduction of the external elements of Al-Qaeda and Iran that really caused this mission very nearly to fail.'[21] Such an admission reveals how the adoption of a proxy war strategy even by non-superpower states such as Iran can be effectively utilized as a mechanism of maximizing interest and circumventing the risks associated with direct intervention.

Non-State Actors and Proxy Wars

As the Iranian case highlights, although states may be the primary instigators of proxy wars, the entire phenomenon rests
in large part upon the co-opting of non-state actors into the
process of undertaking indirect modes of intervention. An
understanding of proxy war based on an assumption of an
exclusively state-based benefactor and a perpetually non-state
proxy is too static.[22] This overlooks the fluidity between the two
roles that states and non-state actors have developed, especially
over the last decade. Contemporary history is replete with examples of non-state actors fulfilling the roles of proxy war actors.
Foremost amongst these have been actors in the Middle East,
namely Hizballah through its relationship with Syria and Iran.

Hizballah emerged from the crucible of the Lebanese Civil
War to become one of the most prominent paramilitary Shia
groups in the predominantly Sunni Arab world. With the
1982 Israeli invasion of Lebanon as its catalyst, Hizballah
became a crucial proxy for neighbouring states, especially
Syria, who sought to defend their interests within Lebanon.
In 1989, Syria and Lebanon signed the Taif Agreement which
consolidated the secular nature of the Lebanese state, legis-
lated for Syria's role within it, and called for the disarming
of paramilitary groups. This last protocol forced Hizballah
to seek some arrangement from Syria to preserve its status.
Mindful of the realpolitik of the region, Syria came to an
agreement with Hizballah that allowed it to maintain its
weapons, in large part so it could preserve an armed non-state
ally as leverage against Israel in the ongoing dispute over the
Golan Heights. Eventually, by the mid-1990s, Hizballah had
become an autonomous actor within Lebanese politics, with
Syrian acquiescence. After he came to power in 2000, Syrian
President Bashar al-Asad forged a close personal bond with
Hizballah leader Hassan Nasrallah, cementing a seeming

symbiosis between the state and its non-state proxy. So close had they become that, in Emile El-Hokayem's words, their 'vital resources and an indispensable political sponsorship elevated Hizballah'.[23]

But it was not only with Syria that Hizballah built links. Their ties with Iran led to much international speculation that the Israeli invasion of Lebanon in the summer of 2006 was masking a wider proxy war between the United States and Iran, with the Israeli Defence Force (IDF) and Hizballah as convenient surrogate proxies in the wider struggle for the control of the direction of Middle Eastern politics.[24] Ever since Hizballah's creation in 1982, its fighters had received training in both Lebanon and Iran from the Iranian Revolutionary Guard (IRG). The IRG had also been a primary conduit for weapons supplies. Furthermore, Iran supplied a significant amount of money in order to allow Hizballah to fulfil both its paramilitary activities and its social provision tasks, estimated to be to the tune of tens of millions of US dollars per year.[25] The US-led invasion of Iraq in March 2003 provided further opportunities for Iran, as already discussed, to expand its proxy war strategy. Yet what remains significant is that Hizballah was utilized as a key proxy inside Iraq too. By November 2003, US and Israeli intelligence reports indicated that Iran was orchestrating the import of Hizballah fighters from Lebanon into Iraq as a mode of undermining the American occupation.[26]

It was not just with Hizballah that Iran and Syria were attempting to cement state/non-state relations in the crucible of Middle Eastern political violence. Attempts to influence the Israel–Palestine conflict by proxy resulted in mutual assistance to Hamas, the most powerful militia group in the occupied territories. Hamas confirmed in 2008 that the Iranian Revolutionary Guard had trained 300 of its fighters and had been doing so since the Israelis had pulled out of

the Gaza Strip in 2005. In addition, Syria had also reportedly trained over 700 Hamas fighters over the same period in
an effort to harness the group as a proxy ally against Israel.[27]
One Hamas commander commented on the level of training
disseminated by the Iranians: 'They [Hamas fighters] come
home with more abilities than we need . . . such as high-tech
capabilities, knowledge about rockets, sniping and fighting
tactics like the ones used by Hizballah.'[28] In short, Iran had
been using both Hamas and Hizballah as proxies to foment
a two-front war for Israel, from Lebanon and from within the
occupied Palestinian territories.

Yet the proxy–benefactor relationships that Hizballah forged
with Syria and Iran were uneasy ones, largely due to divergent
political agendas and a growing sense of autonomy. Although
by the end of the 1990s Syria had accrued distinct regional
leverage and gained an upper hand in dealing with Hizballah,
by the mid-2000s the relationship broke down as Hizballah
asserted more independence. It was from their power bases in
southern Lebanon that they provoked Israel into invading in the
summer of 2006. The resultant stalemate raised Hizballah's
standing in the Arab world, shrugging off its non-state proxy
label as it forged a greater level of self-sufficiency. Furthermore,
despite long-standing Iranian assistance, Hizballah over the
last decade has fiercely protected its political and paramilitary
autonomy from Tehran and has assiduously prevented a picture of subservience from being painted.

Another key illustration of how non-state proxies can
develop autonomous sources of funding or weapons in order
to outgrow the relationship with their original state benefactor is the Lashkae-i-Taiba (LeT) terrorist group. They achieved
sporadic success in striking targets inside India and Kashmir
with the tacit assistance of the Pakistani Inter-Services
Intelligence agency (ISI). The LeT became, as Ryan Clarke has
argued, 'a vital component of Islamabad's regional strategy'.[29]

Yet, in the early part of this decade, the LeT began to develop a more nuanced pan-Islamic political programme that transcended the Kashmir-oriented scope of Pakistan's original proxy deal. By transferring its cooperation away from the ISI to other sub-state Islamist groups, including al-Qaeda, the LeT no longer remains a surrogate force of Pakistan, but has perhaps become a surrogate force for the wider Islamist terror network spearheaded by al-Qaeda – an example of how one non-state actor can be utilized as a proxy surrogate by another non-state actor. It also serves as a showcase for how proxy relationships are not infinite and, tellingly, can be brought to an end by proxy group maturity and autonomy, not just by benefactors terminating funding or provisions.

Ariel Ahram has reminded us how 'late-developing states' in the global south have willingly co-opted militias into their security apparatus in order to 'organize institutions of coercion' instead of reverting to traditional bureaucracies of violence.[30] The prevalence of state-sponsored militias, such as the Janjaweed in Sudan, the Autodefensas in Columbia, and the Interahamwe in Rwanda, has opened up new avenues for states wishing to fight proxy wars even on their own soil, be it for interest or ideology-motivated reasons of ethnic repression, anti-terrorism or the suppression of irredentist movements. Seeing state-sponsored militias as surrogate forces helps us place proxy wars in an intra-state context alongside its more frequent inter-state mode. This is amply demonstrated by the dynamics of proxy involvement in the protracted conflicts across East Africa over the past few decades.

Case Study: East African Wars and Non-State Proxies

Between 1986 and 1999, Sudan and Uganda were engaging non-state proxies to fight an undeclared war in each other's territory. Sudan harnessed the millenarian Lord's Resistance Army (LRA) that had been fighting the regime of Yoweri Museveni across northern Uganda. Concomitantly, the Ugandan government was backing the Sudanese People's Liberation Army (SPLA) as a mode of undermining the Sudanese government's control over the south of their country. Yet, as Gerard Prunier has emphasized, this proxy war has actually been fought in large part on the territory of the neighbouring Democratic Republic of Congo (DRC), formerly Zaire.[31] Within the DRC, Sudan helped foster the Allied Democratic Force (ADF) as an umbrella grouping of anti-Museveni forces. This set the scene for a protracted conflict and provides a crucial example of how non-state proxies can be utilized to fulfil a state's strategic goals.

Sudan itself had been the scene of multiple proxy interventions in the 1960s when Israel armed anti-Islamist movements, while Khartoum was receiving backing from Moscow in the face of American support for the neighbouring regime of Ethiopia's Haile Selassi. This arrangement ended in 1974 when Selassi was overthrown and replaced by the communist Dergue regime, which soon received Soviet backing. The US switched its support to Sudan whom it furnished with over $2 billion in arms to fight Islamist and communist rebels.[32] Yet, as the Cold War progressed, Sudan and Uganda became embroiled in a covert proxy war against each other that is noteworthy in part because of the use not of another state's military as their chosen proxies but of non-state actors.

The origins of the Sudanese–Ugandan conflict were politico-religious. The coming to power in Uganda of the pro-American Yoweri Museveni had prompted fears in Khartoum that the SPLA would have a new ally based on a misguided assumption as to the closeness of the personal relationship between Museveni and the SPLA leader John Garang. The conflict intensified in 1989 when the National Islamic Front

(NIF), led by Dr Hassan al-Turabi, backed a military coup in Sudan. The new Islamist junta aimed to Islamize the Great Lakes region, including the predominantly Christian parts of Uganda and southern Sudan.

Ethiopian support for the SPLA, which had proved one of its most fruitful benefactors, ended in autumn 1991 when Colonel Mengistu's regime fell. Soon afterwards, the SPLA degenerated into internecine violence. This was a blow to Ugandan designs on disrupting the Sudanese government. By 1994, it appeared that Sudan was having more success in assisting its main proxy force inside Uganda, the LRA. Within a year, Sudan had recruited nearly 2,000 additional guerrillas to the ranks of the LRA and armed them to such an extent that they posed a distinct threat to the Ugandan government.[33] Also by 1994, the Sudanese government had gained permission from President Mobutu of Zaire to run supply convoys to the LRA in western Uganda through his country. It also allowed the Sudanese to adopt other anti-Museveni proxies in western Uganda, namely, the Western Nile Bank Liberation Front (WNBLF) and the Uganda Muslim Liberation Army (UMLA).

The second half of 1995 saw both Sudan and Uganda take greater control of their non-state proxies. In coalition with the WNBLF, the Sudanese army wrestled control of two towns close to the Ugandan border in August of that year. In retaliation, the Ugandans launched a joint operation in conjunction with the SPLA against LRA strongholds actually inside Sudanese territory that September. A major escalation of the conflict ensued in 1996 as the defeat of each other's respective proxy forces became major defence priorities. Ugandan President Museveni authorized his troops to cross into Zaire in order to intercept ADF fighters, while the Sudanese were simultaneously conducting air resupply missions to the LRA inside Uganda.[34]

Ultimately, this escalated conflict, facilitated primarily by the utilization of non-state proxy forces, resulted in a seeming defeat for the Sudanese proxies, who retreated from their Zaire sanctuary by early 1997. This, however, did not mark the ending of hostilities or the abandonment of a proxy war strategy. In 1998, the Sudanese government began building a coalition of other non-state forces, including those from Chad, to act as a proxy force inside the Zaire (which after May 1997 was called the Democratic Republic of Congo (DRC)). A 'peace agreement' between Sudan, Uganda and the DRC was signed in April 1999, which in essence removed the proxy component of the conflict.[35] Despite simmering tensions after this accord was signed, this complex regional conflict displays the prevalence non-state proxies can play in shaping national and indeed regional wars if co-opted by states to act on their behalf within the borders of a neighbouring state. Indeed, this protracted series of East African proxy wars harnessed a wide variety of methods by which to wage such a conflict. The next chapter looks in detail at exactly how proxy wars are fought and by what means.

CHAPTER FOUR

How are Proxy Wars Fought?

There is not one uniform way in which proxy wars are fought. The utilization of various proxy war strategies are a long-standing phenomenon in the history of warfare. As such, we are able to perceive a multiplicity of approaches in exactly how they have been undertaken. This chapter will explore the main components of a proxy war strategy and break down each facet, including the provision of manpower (via surrogates); the delivery of materiel (such as weapons); financial assistance; and non-military means (mechanisms of so-called 'soft power').

Provision of Manpower

Proxy wars are similar to most other forms of war inasmuch as the provision of manpower is often seen as essential to the outcome. Since proxy interventions occur within other categories of war, such as a civil war, benefactors usually perceive the need to provide help in terms of indirectly bolstering the number of 'boots on the ground', via a surrogate force or non-combatant military 'advisers'. Significant debates about the meaning and impact of troop levels on other typologies of war, in particular counter-insurgency, have been rife as a result of the wars in Afghanistan and Iraq. Counter-insurgency theorists have forwarded contending hypotheses surrounding the link between force size and conflict outcome, including the importance of the ratio between insurgent and counter-insurgent, and between population size and counter-insurgent.[1] Although no parallel debate has taken place in relation to proxy wars (such as debates about the force ratio of proxies to enemy combatants), the centrality of manpower to how proxy wars have been fought in the past and today is critical.

The USSR made prolific use of manpower as a form of proxy assistance. As the Cold War progressed, they permitted their military advisers in proxy conflicts to engage in an ever more expansive array of activities. Routine technical assistance and the giving and receiving of intelligence material was a repertoire soon expanded to include operational planning for foreign militaries (as undertaken during the Yemeni Civil War), the organization of troop transportation (as seen during the Yom Kippur war on behalf of the Egyptians) and distribution of weaponry (as witnessed during the Angolan Civil War).[2]

By 1978, more than 40,000 Cuban troops were acting as Soviet surrogates in proxy conflicts across the Third World.[3] At the height of Cuban involvement in the Angolan Civil War in early 1976, advisers from Havana were being flown into the country at a rate of 200 a day.[4] Cuban military personnel had become the favoured surrogate force during Soviet proxy wars. During the Cold War, Cubans were deployed to Libya, Yemen, Angola, Ethiopia, Benin, Sierra Leone, Uganda, Equatorial Guinea, Grenada and Nicaragua.[5] However, the use of Cuban surrogate forces was not exclusive. Egyptian pilots had been trained to fly Soviet planes during the Nigerian Civil War, while Czechoslovakian troops and military advisers had been utilized on numerous occasions in African war zones.[6] On occasion, though in far fewer numbers than the Cubans, the Soviets relied on deployments of East German specialists, primarily from the State Security Service (SSD), in order to help build the internal security and intelligence capabilities of Third World allies such as Angola, Ethiopia and Libya.[7] Crucially, the Soviets themselves were not averse to sending their own military advisers to war zones as overt agents of proxy intervention. Just over 50,000 such personnel were deployed by proxy to various war zones between 1955 and 1980, while an additional 50,000 foreign military personnel were trained by the Soviets within the USSR itself.[8]

A major task that the provision of manpower can fulfil is a coup/counter-coup function. On several occasions, the USSR sponsored proxy forces in the Third World that were utilized to protect allied regimes from coup threats. For example, in June 1966, the president of Congo-Brazzaville (modern-day Congo), Massama Debat, was given an armed guard by Cuban surrogate forces when the Congolese army seized control of the capital as part of a military coup. This Cuban protection, and the threat of an escalation of Cuban manpower in support of Debat, eventually led to the collapse of the coup attempt.[9]

Provision of Materiel

The supplying of military materiel, such as arms, ammunition and other military technology, by benefactors to their chosen proxies is the prime way for benefactors to get others to do the fighting for them. It is the provision of means to ensure a specific end without having to engage in the messy business of war-fighting themselves. The delivery of weapons is the most potent symbol of proxy war as arm's-length conflict engagement. Symptomatic of such symbolism was the British Foreign Office's reference back in 1948 to their proxy intervention in the Chinese Civil War as merely 'keeping a foot in the door', after their provision of 1,000 guns to the beleaguered government of Chiang Kai-shek despite the existence of multinational non-intervention agreements.[10] The supply of such weapons does not just buy arms for the proxies. It also buys a stake in the conflict outcome for the benefactor, and ties the two parties together.

Between 1965 and 1972, the USSR exported approximately $6.5billion worth of weapons to countries in the Third World, nearly half of which went to North Vietnam during the war against the Americans.[11] As the 1970s progressed, the Soviet approach to proxy wars shifted. Hitherto, the Kremlin had been content with supplying relatively modest amounts of arms to client regimes (the exception being the shipments undertaken during the Korean and Vietnam Wars). But, during the mid-to-late 1970s, the USSR adopted a more aggressive stance in relation to indirect conflict engagement that manifested itself primarily through the significant expansion of arms provision to proxy allies. This arguably was driven as much by an increased strategic rivalry with China as it was with the US. Soviet arms shipments to fellow communist – and sympathetic non-communist – countries increased noticeably as the Sino–Soviet split, when combined with the process of US-Soviet detente, pushed geostrategic tensions into a frenzy of proxy activity. The CIA estimated that, between 1974 and 1978, the USSR exported nearly $15 billion worth of war-fighting equipment, including tanks, fighter jets and bombers, to proxy war zones around the world.[12]

The Americans were not to be left behind in the Cold War effort to maximize proxy war strategies. By 1962, the CIA was spending $2 million a year on training foreign internal security forces in counter-subversion techniques. Up to that point, it was estimated that around 1,450 personnel across the Third World had received such CIA training. President Kennedy, in effect, placed the US on a perpetual proxy war footing. Testament to this was the establishment in November 1962 of the Office for Public Safety (OPS) to oversee the police training in internal security assistance missions. By the following year, nearly 200 American police advisory personnel were deployed across thirty different countries, training over 1 million members of foreign security forces.[13]

Provision of Financial Assistance

If the motives for sending money to a warring faction in an existing conflict are not explicitly humanitarian or for development reasons and are perceived to be for the broader strategic reasons of furthering a war aim, then this can be seen as a form of proxy intervention. Some proxy war benefactors have taken this financial motive and utilized huge amounts of their economic resources to assist a chosen proxy. For example, one estimate of total Soviet financial provision to Third World proxies (*excluding* its foremost proxies in Cuba, Vietnam and North Korea), between 1955 and 1980, puts the figure at around $51billion.[14]

Contemporary developments in the world system, prompted by the influences of globalization, have ensured that the provision of money in a proxy war setting need no longer necessarily be restricted to an understanding of financing surrogate forces who have been physically deployed to war zones. The emergence of transnational insurgent groups, such as al-Qaeda, has altered how proxy wars can be fought and financed. The increased development of attacks constituting 'propaganda of the deed' with a global audience in mind has allowed contemporary insurgents to harness the support of networked diasporas around the world. Elements of these diasporas invest their support and money in myriad causes and groups that work towards overarching goals in line with their perceived interests or ideology, regardless of their proximity to the conflict. In effect, this has meant that insurgent groups are increasingly acting as proxies not for benefactor states, but for dispersed ethnic communities and coalesced political forces from around the world who invest their faith and money in perpetuating ethno-religious conflict.[15] The same was also true of segments of the Irish-American diaspora at the height of the Northern Irish 'Troubles' in the early 1970s, who decided to contribute to the struggle in the 'old country' by fundraising to facilitate shipments of weapons to the Provisional Irish Republican Army (PIRA), mainly via the Northern Irish Aid Committee (Noraid).[16]

Financial assistance is undertaken in many cases for the purposes of allowing allies to train security forces that can then be utilized as proxies by the benefactor. This was a primary use of such money during the Cold War. For example, the Pentagon spent $17.2million in 1962 alone on military assistance to just six countries: South Vietnam, Iran, Costa Rica, Nicaragua, Panama and the Philippines.[17]

Provision of Non-Military Assistance

Joseph Nye famously conceptualized the notion of 'soft power' in world politics as constituting 'the ability to get what you want through attraction rather than coercion or payments. It arises out of a country's culture, political ideals, and policies.'[18] Nye's analysis of soft power is useful to engage with when assessing forms of influence other than traditionally coercive military mechanisms, primarily because it requires us to assess the means by which proxy forms of intervention can be sought. The fundamentally indirect nature of proxy wars mean that they need not automatically be categorized as a perpetual 'hard power' type of intervention. Military assistance is not always offered. Admittedly, coercion may be an underlying current in many such wars, but that does not discount the possibility of a proxy's willingness to seek a benefactor's help because of the attractiveness of their political worldview, or indeed a benefactor emphasizing the appeal (or legitimacy) of their particular ideology as a source of attracting allies in strategically important areas. For example, political encouragement via the nurturing of Marxist-Leninist vanguard parties became an important additional strand in the Kremlin's attempts to consolidate its influence in the Third World during the Cold War.[19] The marketing of both communism and liberal democracy during the mid-twentieth century by their respective superpower champions became integral strands of soft-power influence as they attempted to shape the ideological preferences of other states in the world. This can therefore be seen as a catalyst to the creation of benefactor–proxy relationships.

When analysing forms of power, it is important for us not to become exclusively concerned with conceptual additions of verbs like 'hard' and 'soft' as this ensures a deconstruction solely of the *means* by which power is rendered and often ignores the *ends* to which it is pursued. As Joseph Nye himself acknowledges, power in pure terms is 'the ability to influence the behaviour of others to get the outcomes one wants'.[20]

Categorizations of 'hard' or 'soft' rest on an analysis of the first part of Nye's definition (modes of influence), whereas a focus on the second part (outcomes) speaks to all forms of power. Proxy wars, whether conducted overtly, covertly, with or without surrogates, are all essentially undertaken to get the outcome the benefactor wants. More often than not, this has included the resort to 'hard' power modes of intervention, such as the provision of weapons, but infrequently it has included the provision of non-military assistance. This is one reason why the case study of US military support to the 'Anbar Awakening' in Iraq in 2006 is included at the end of this chapter. Not only does it demonstrate the multiple forms of support that a proxy war can include, but it also highlights Nye's point about soft power being co-optive, revealing how an eventual proxy (the 'Sons of Iraq') actually invited the US military to act as their benefactor in their effort to rid Anbar province of the influence of al-Qaeda in Iraq.[21]

The provision of non-military assistance can, on occasion, be primarily constitutive of symbolism and contain no real material value. This has manifested itself through the threat to adopt a proxy war strategy in order to act as a deterrent against other states intervening, or as a warning to an incumbent regime to not act in a particular way (thus not necessarily fulfilling Nye's criteria of a 'soft-power' mechanism because of the reliance on coercion). Back in 1998, for example, American congressional exasperation at Saddam Hussein's repeated breaches of UN resolutions led the 105th Republican-led Congress to pass the Iraq Liberation Act, which allocated President Bill Clinton the right to disperse $97 million worth of military equipment to opponents of Saddam's regime within Iraq.[22] Although President Clinton signed this Bill into law (thus establishing regime change in Iraq as a tenet of American foreign policy years before the 9/11 attacks and President George W. Bush's 'Axis of Evil'), he 'had no intention of arming Iraqi insurgents and starting a proxy war' in Iraq.[23] Clinton had clearly acknowledged that an outright proxy war would be unfeasible, yet the potency of threatening to start one held a symbolic function for his administration and served both as a warning to Saddam Hussein and as a tokenistic gesture of solidarity with Saddam's victims.

Alternatively, the provision of non-military assistance can take the form of assistance in spreading propaganda to aid the cause of a chosen proxy. This manifestation of indirect 'information warfare' helps change opinions, winning the 'hearts and minds' of local populations, either through appeals to the legitimacy of their ideology/party or, more commonly, through the discrediting of opponents and planting of disinformation. Returning briefly to the case of Angola that we looked at in chapter 3, the CIA helped bolster their proxy ally UNITA by getting stories placed in the largest newspapers in neighbouring countries Zaire and Zambia that reported on how UNITA fighters had captured a certain city and detained numerous Soviet advisers. The key to this strategy was that this battle never actually took place. It was a deceit aimed at boosting regional interpretations of UNITA's strength and likely chances of emerging as victor in the civil war.[24]

By perceiving the multiple means by which proxy wars can be fought, we can see how benefactors go about securing their desired outcome in conflicts. On occasion, benefactors resort to utilizing one form, or a combination, of the provisions discussed above. It is worthwhile reflecting upon two cases in particular that highlight how all of the forms of support – materiel, manpower, finance and non-military – can be harnessed at the same time. First, let us explore how the so-called 'Anbar Awakening' – a movement widely perceived to have significantly aided the American military turn the tide against al-Qaeda insurgents in Iraq – came to manifest a proxy war strategy at the heart of the US campaign there. Second, we will turn to the case of Afghanistan during the Soviet occupation of 1979–89, and the waging of a proxy war by the United States in support of the mujahedeen fighters.

Case Study 1: The 'Anbar Awakening'

The case of the 'Anbar Awakening' is yet another example of how an indirect proxy war strategy can sit alongside a direct conventional war in the same battle space. This case illustrates how a state (the US) used a non-state actor (the Sunni tribes in Anbar province) to undermine another non-state actor (al-Qaeda in Iraq), by co-opting them as paramilitary proxies and providing them with the provisions to achieve a mutually desired goal.

Two years after the initial invasion of Iraq in 2003 by the 400,000-strong twenty-seven-nation 'coalition of the willing', Iraq was in the grip of vicious insurgent violence, driven by contending militia groups of differing ethnic, religious and tribal affiliations. One of the most potent, and violent, of these groups was a multinational franchise that labelled itself al-Qaeda in Iraq (AQI), led by the Jordanian Abu Musab al-Zarqawi. AQI had found a foothold in the 'Sunni Triangle' in central and western Iraq, centred around Anbar province, which the Americans had taken to calling 'the Triangle of Death'. Dedicating itself to casting the coalition forces out of Iraq through the undertaking of continuous sniper, mortar and Improvised Explosive Device (IED) attacks, AQI had found the tribal sheikhs of Anbar a natural ally in the battle against the occupying force.

By 2005, however, the rise of AQI in Anbar began to unsettle the previously friendly tribal leaders for three main reasons: there was a clash of goals (the transnational Islamism of AQI versus the localized power-based objectives of the tribes); a clash of resource requirements (AQI had begun muscling in on the tribal monopolies of smuggling and banditry); and a clash of values (AQI's violent imposition of its interpretation of *sharia* law on tribal areas, and attempts at forced marriage between AQI fighters and tribal women, without the sheikh's consent).

As a backlash against this perceived abuse of AQI's power, a relatively minor sheikh from Ramadi, Sattar al-Rishawi, formed an umbrella group for Anbar's various tribal leaders in 2006, and named it the Anbar Salvation Council (ASC). The ASC reached out to the US military and politicians in order to secure both 'hard' and 'soft' assistance in ridding Anbar of AQI's influence. The Americans duly obliged. Al-Rishawi was appointed Anbar's counter-insurgency coordinator, and his growing band of militiamen, who came to be known as the 'Sons of Iraq', were co-opted as an 'Emergency Response Unit' by the US military. The Americans had found a willing proxy to step in and take the fight to one of their most entrenched and violent insurgent opponents, abrogating themselves to a large extent of the human cost of sending in large numbers of troops to search and destroy pockets of AQI resistance.

The 'Sons of Iraq' soon became, in the words of one US Marine deployed to Iraq, 'an amazing force multiplier'.[25] The US military ensured that they were armed, trained and paid to act as efficient surrogates for them in Anbar. At the height of the group's strength, in 2008, there were 103,000 'Sons of Iraq' on the US military payroll, costing the Americans $30 million in monthly wages.[26] The vast majority were disconcerted Sunnis, some of whom had previously been members of anti-American insurgent groups. But, under the rubric of a new approach to ameliorating the violence in some of the most volatile areas of Iraq, the Americans were happy to make allied proxies out of their former enemies. According to two American officers involved in strengthening what became known as the 'Awakening' in Anbar: 'The situation was a winner any way you looked at it. The tribes saw that instead of being the hunted, they could become the hunters, with well trained, paid, and equipped security forces.'[27] In some cases, the fighters traded their previous weapons with the Americans in exchange for newer, better guns, while favoured tribal leaders were paid additional bonuses as a reward for their loyalty by the CIA.[28] American diplomatic support was also offered as a 'soft-power' means of shoring up tribal support, with President Bush himself taking a meeting and photo-opportunity with al-Rishawi in an effort to legitimize their new proxies as actors in the politics of the new Iraq.

The results of this proxy war strategy were tangible. Ramadi, the provincial capital of Anbar, saw its tally of attacks reduced substantially in the wake of the rise of the 'Anbar Awakening'.[29] But that is not to say that the proxy war was without risk. The Americans at first decided not to inform the Shia government of Nouri al-Maliki of the policy of turning

Sunni tribes into proxy surrogates. When the profile of the 'Sons of Iraq' became too high to hide, al-Maliki instinctively feared that the 'Awakening' fighters were not an American proxy in the war against AQI, but were being used as a Sunni proxy to counter-balance Shia political control in Baghdad.[30] Furthermore, as Austin Long has pointed out, the surrogacy of the 'Sons of Iraq' was antithetical to 'the creation of a stable, unified and democratic Iraq' because of the way in which the Americans had armed and empowered a non-democratic, non-state actor without the direct permission of the sovereign Iraqi government.[31] But, as the next case study demonstrates, sometimes the calculus of risk in relation to perceived benefit pushes states in favour of a proxy war strategy anyway.

Case Study 2: America, the Mujahedeen and the Soviet Occupation of Afghanistan, 1979–89

America's proxy war strategy in Afghanistan was summed up by Charles Cogan, one of the CIA's chief operatives in the region, in simple terms: 'we took the means to wage war, put them in the hands of people who could do so, for the purposes for which we agreed'.[32] The first American arms delivery – a shipment of rifles – arrived just fourteen days after the Soviets had invaded Afghanistan on 24 December 1979 in an effort to prop up a crumbling communist regime in Kabul. This swift response by President Jimmy Carter demonstrated the degree of readiness with which he was willing to adopt a proxy war strategy.

Significantly, however, the Carter administration had decided to undertake a proxy intervention in Afghanistan before the Soviet invasion had actually occurred. Hoping to capitalize on growing unrest within the country and further destabilize the communist government, President Carter authorized a budget of $500,000 for the CIA to assist anti-communist rebels in Afghanistan through the provision of radio equipment, medicines and cash during the summer of 1979.[33] Once the invasion did take place, Carter's National Security Advisor, Zbigniew Brzezinski, advocated the adoption of a proxy war strategy based on the principle of making 'Soviet involvement as costly as possible'.[34] The aim, in short, was to create a quagmire by proxy.

The initial Carter administration attempt to boost the credibility of the proxy strategy's 'plausible deniability' manifested itself via payments to the Egyptian government of Anwar Sadat to provide Soviet-made weapons to the mujahedeen so that any traceability back to Washington was minimized.[35] Such efforts to put communist-produced weaponry in the hands of anti-communist rebels in Afghanistan, and so disguise US involvement, also led the CIA to elicit arms purchased from dissident Polish army officers and, significantly, from the Chinese who made large profits on arms sales to the CIA as a means of achieving communist supremacy in the wake of the Sino–Soviet split.[36] By the summer of 1981, the mujahedeen was receiving arms at the rate of two full plane loads per week.[37]

The most significant turning point in America's proxy war in Afghanistan arguably came in March 1985, when President Ronald Reagan signed National Security Decision Directive (NSDD) 166, which authorized the expansion of American aid to the mujahedeen to include 'all means available'.[38] This expansion of the US proxy war included the initiation of intelligence sharing and a fivefold increase in the level of financial aid offered to the Afghan guerrillas, climbing from $122 million in 1984 to $630 million by 1987.[39] But it was the new form of weaponry provided to the mujahedeen that created the most decisive element of this proxy war. This mainly came down to the provision of one weapon in particular: the Stinger surface-to-air missile. One of the greatest perceived weaknesses faced by America's Afghan proxies was the monopoly on air power that the Soviets enjoyed. The effect was almost immediate. Estimates put the total figure of Soviet aircraft shot down by the Stingers at 269.[40] Within two months of the first shipment of Stingers arriving in Afghanistan, the Soviet Politburo had planned and announced an exit strategy for its troops from the country.[41]

Yet the Americans did not restrict themselves to weapons supply. In all, the CIA trained over 50,000 mujahedeen fighters as a means of strengthening the paramilitary potency of their chosen proxy surrogate force.[42] Indeed, assistance to the mujahedeen was not exclusively military in its form. Non-military forms of help were manifested through the sizeable political weight given towards interventionist goals. Groups sprang up in Washington, with the goal of lobbying Congress to increase aid to the mujahedeen and advising on political strategies to advance their cause. Such groups included the Committee for a Free Afghanistan, the Federation for American-Afghan Action, Free the Eagle, and the Freedom Research Foundation.

The US provided nearly $3 billion in covert aid for the Afghan resistance movement between 1979 and 1989. This sum accounted for more than all other American covert operations in the 1980s combined.[43] It is a figure made all the more significant considering that the Saudi Arabian authorities were matching American money dollar for dollar. As a proxy war strategy it was not especially covert, but it retained all the facets of an indirect campaign. As the then CIA Director William Casey acknowledged, the adoption of a proxy war strategy helped mitigate international perceptions of inherent and overbearing American direct intervention: 'Here's the beauty of the Afghan operation ... Usually it looks like the big bad Americans are beating up on the natives. Afghanistan is just the reverse. The Russians are beating up on the little guys. We don't make it our war . . . All we have to do is give them help.'[44] Not making conflicts 'their' wars and giving client groups 'help' to win them is exactly how states have been fighting proxy wars for decades. There is little indication that these inherent characteristics will change in the decades to come. Indeed, as the next chapter will show, there is significant reason to believe that proxy wars will become increasingly prevalent in the entire dynamic of war and conflict in the future.

CHAPTER FIVE

The Future of Proxy War

In an era when the world is in the midst of a global financial downturn and the images of flag-laden coffins on television screens hardens Western attitudes against sending troops abroad, the utilization of proxy forces holds both an economic and political appeal to modern states. Such a market-driven arrangement that seemingly values the lives of one set of soldiers over another may be undesirable, even repugnant, yet as the pressures of new emergent threats stretch the capabilities and resilience of liberal states, the nature of war-fighting will adapt in line with the processes of globalization. As the twenty-first century unfolds, the willingness of citizens to voluntarily join ever-shrinking national armies is declining, the cost of cutting-edge military technology is rising and, particularly in the wake of the protracted and costly wars in Iraq and Afghanistan, the appetite for repeated expeditionary counterinsurgency warfare is diminished. These symptoms, however, are present despite an inevitable desire amongst states not to lose or cede strategic interest. When combined, these coexisting predilections are not necessarily mutually exclusive. Arguably, it can be foreseen that the increased use of proxy forces will circumvent the issues of low military recruitment rates, public aversion to casualties and squeezed defence budgets, without states manifestly surrendering their interests vested in a particular conflict or region. As Philip Bobbitt argued in 2003: 'In the future, the use of local proxy armies can offer . . . an economic alternative to more expensive standing armies . . . [and] could provide the indispensable element of ground control without risking American lives to the same degree as US ground forces.'[1] The signposts certainly point in this direction. Yet whether it is a desirable road to go down remains distinctly questionable.

The centrality of proxy wars to the future of conflict is something policymakers and military leaders are already preparing for. A 2010 report for the UK Ministry of Defence, entitled *Future Character of Conflict*, posited how wars in the coming decades will 'be categorized as a mosaic of adversaries, threats and responses. Our adversaries will comprise states, non-states and proxies; they will cooperate where they see mutual benefit.'[2] The prescience of this observation may well become apparent as a result of the coalescence of four major changes in the nature of modern warfare and international relations, which the rest of this chapter will analyse in turn: the emergence of a contemporary 'Vietnam Syndrome' which has decreased public and political appetite in the West for large-scale counter-insurgency 'quagmires' against a backdrop of a global recession; the rise in prominence and importance of Private Military Companies (PMCs) to contemporary war-fighting; the increasing use of cyberspace as a platform from which to indirectly wage war; and the ascent of China as a world superpower.

A War on Terror Syndrome?

The draining of public support for foreign wars and the political reluctance to deploy large numbers of troops abroad in the future formed the essential characteristics of the 'Vietnam Syndrome' that impacted upon American foreign policy from the early 1970s. Yet the result was not isolationism or acquiescence to Soviet interests in the Third World. Instead, successive American administrations resorted to proxy warfare as a means of maximizing interest and ideology without exacerbating the side effects of the syndrome. It is little surprise that some of the most significant American proxy war efforts of the Cold War, in Angola in the mid-1970s and Afghanistan throughout the 1980s, came in the wake of the ignominious withdrawal from South East Asia. This post-Vietnam resort to indirect intervention perhaps holds key signifiers for how the US will again reassess ways to maintain its strategic initiatives after withdrawal from the recent long and costly wars in Iraq and Afghanistan. Indeed, some commentators have already gone as far as to advocate the adoption of an overt proxy war stance in relation to al-Qaeda. In January 2002, just three months after the invasion of Afghanistan, the centre-right think tank the CATO Institute published a paper suggesting that America could achieve its long-term and far-reaching goals by turning the War on Terror into a strategic proxy war. The paper posited that by funding, arming and training 'effective and reasonable local actors' in countries facing Islamist threats, then the US could get 'the most bang for its buck . . . while at the same time lessening the chances that the United States will be a lightning rod for retaliatory terrorism'.[3] This bold assertion certainly cut to the core of proxy wars' base appeal (keep your own hands clean while others bloody theirs for you), yet it remains unreflective in its essential contention that the US needs to effectively return to its Cold War mindset of 'my enemy's enemy is my friend'. The scope for 'blowback' (unintended future consequences of foreign policy actions) remain incredibly high, as the Cold War experience demonstrated[4] – most notably, with the efforts to fund and arm a seemingly useful and conservative band of Islamic resistance fighters in order to bog down the Soviet Army in Afghanistan in the 1980s. Proxy wars undeniably have a strategic allure to them; however, their long-term consequences, as discussed fully in the concluding chapter, can be harmful to both the original benefactor and the proxy themselves.

The state of war and conflict in the modern world is in flux. Both the methods of war-fighting and the actors involved in the process are changing. This evolution brings with it the possibility for academics, policymakers and military practitioners alike to theorize and conceptualize about the nature of warfare at the dawn of the twenty-first century. Colin Gray has advanced three broad propositions about the characteristics of violent conflict in our times: '(a) the twenty-first century will be another bloody century; (b) war and strategy will continue as ever, albeit in new guises . . . and (c) the insecurity or security narrative of the century will be amply explainable with reference to the genius of Thucydides' "fear, honour and interest"'.[5] The 'new guises' of war and strategy that Gray alludes to are perhaps ones that will not readily be seen, cloaked as they may be in indirect modes of intervention and arm's-length recruitment of proxy forces.

The key signifiers that point towards 'another bloody century', from the perspective of this book, include the aforementioned diminishing thirst for asymmetric wars with a parallel commitment to large-scale nation-building projects, contextualized within a global recession and inevitable defence budget cuts across the Western world. Indeed, we are already witnessing the effects of these intertwined themes. In January 2012, the Pentagon announced plans for a leaner US military and a reduction in the US defence budget. In his forward to this defence review, President Obama explicitly tied together the issues of financial chaos and military cutbacks: 'We must put our fiscal house in order here at home and renew our long-term economic strength . . . [This] mandates reductions in federal spending, including defense spending.'[6] This would include Pentagon budget cuts of approximately $450 billion, while engendering a 10–15 per cent reduction in the size of the US Army and Marine Corps over the coming decade.[7] The review does, however, crucially leave the door open for the potential future adoption of proxy wars if and when reductions in the defence budget and/or the rise of an aggressive Chinese military necessitates more indirect means by which to protect American interests. Statements such as 'we will develop innovative, low-cost and small footprint approaches to achieve our security objectives', and 'the US military will invest as required to ensure its ability to operate effectively in anti-access and area denial (A2/AD) environments', indicate an awareness of the possibilities of harnessing proxy war strategies in areas where direct military intervention is either too costly or too risky in the years ahead.[8]

In addition to these budgetary signposts, we can include other trends whose fluctuation should remain closely monitored for an indication of the expansive appeal of proxy wars in the future. Foremost amongst these include levels of foreign military assistance that states allocate (particularly when viewed in comparison to levels of domestic military expenditure), and, perhaps most crucially of all, the increase in the number of contracts being awarded to PMCs to fulfil security functions on behalf of states.

Private Military Companies as Proxy War-Wagers of the Future

A greater congruence between the military actions of states and the use of PMCs (or 'coalitions of the billing' as Christopher Coker has pithily labelled them[9]) has become a defining hallmark of contemporary security policy in the West. Engaging in activities such as weapons procurement, police training, intelligence gathering and the close personal protection of civilian leaders, PMCs have operated in a wide range of countries since the end of the Cold War, including

Angola, the Democratic Republic of Congo, Ethiopia, Eritrea, Liberia, Sierra Leone, Kashmir, the Balkans, Afghanistan and Iraq. The bulk of PMC personnel are former members of national militaries, predominantly those of the US, UK, France, Israel and South Africa, with 80 per cent of all PMCs registered in either the US or the UK.[10] However, no census of PMC operatives in conflict zones is undertaken, therefore obfuscating a full analysis of their numbers and influence.[11]

The end of the Cold War prompted governments around the globe to downsize their armies to the collective tune of approximately 6 million personnel during the 1990s.[12] Significant numbers of these highly skilled individuals were therefore readily transferable into the private sector. The rise of 'failed states' caused in part by post-Cold War power vacuums ensured an increased demand for security provision to match the parallel rise in supply of personnel. When seen alongside wider changes to the very nature of warfare itself (via the high-tech advances made during the post-Cold War 'revolution in military affairs') and the broader socio-economic acceptance in the West of privatized goods and services, a permissive environment had been created to such an extent by the late 1990s that PMCs were acting, in David Shearer's words, 'as foreign policy proxies for governments unable or unwilling to play a direct and open role'.[13] This explanation cuts to the core of why PMCs are poised to become key proxy war-wagers in the future. Not only do they fulfil the critical function of minimizing risk for states eager to still protect interests or ideology, but they provide additional economic benefits to a form of war caricatured as 'warfare on the cheap', inasmuch as PMCs have lower start-up and running costs than national military deployments, alongside the absence of redundancy or pension provision states have to pay private contractors, unlike their soldiers.[14]

Yet, perhaps most significantly, they circumvent the

difficulties created by a latter-day Vietnam Syndrome (as discussed above). There are no repatriation ceremonies for dead private military contractors, no flag-draped coffins, no public recrimination at fatalities. Thus, the political risk that states run in deploying their own troops to foreign wars is drastically reduced when they permit a PMC to accept the risk on their behalf instead – and PMCs are seemingly willing to accept this risk. As Tim Spicer, the founder of the controversial PMC Sandline, argued at the height of the humanitarian interventionist moment in the late 1990s: 'live footage on CNN of United States soldiers being killed in Somalia has had staggering effects on the willingness of governments to commit to foreign conflicts. We fill the gap.'[15] The degeneration of the wars in Afghanistan and Iraq into protracted counter-insurgency conflicts has arguably reignited such reluctant sentiment in the West towards deploying troops on a large scale again in the near future. Peter Singer has argued that the appeal of PMCs to American administrations lies with the Executive branch's desire to occasionally evade Congressional restrictions on troop deployment and avoid the political costs of having to call up high numbers of reservists. So, for example, during the Bosnian crisis in the late 1990s, Singer estimates that President Clinton's reliance on PMCs resulted in the Pentagon deploying 9,000 fewer troops to the country than they would otherwise have had to.[16] Indeed, such a trend has been prevalent during the War on Terror. Erik Prince, founder of another infamous PMC, Blackwater, bluntly asserted in a 2010 interview that he had put his company 'at the CIA's disposal' on many occasions. Between 2001 and 2009, Blackwater received over $1.5 billion in US government contracts to fulfil key functions for the American intelligence community. Their training headquarters in North Carolina saw 30,000 personnel pass through its facilities annually during that time.[17] Christopher Kinsey has argued that so close have some PMCs become to their home nation governments that they have in effect become proxies by default. He highlights how the American PMC Military Professional Resources Inc (MPRI) developed such a close working relationship with the Pentagon that it had fully shaped its provision to suit Department of Defense needs, providing training for both US forces and foreign forces on behalf of the US. As Kinsey states, the Pentagon-MPRI connection is a prime example 'of how a PMC can enable a government to attain its foreign policy objectives without first having to secure congressional approval, and with the knowledge that if things go wrong the government can distance itself from involvement'.[18] The use of PMCs as proxy war-fighters for Western governments has already begun.

So reliant upon PMC assistance has the American military become that, in the opinion of one former PMC contractor, 'the US Army would break down without them'.[19] Indeed, an analysis of the role PMCs have played in the recent 'wars of terror' in Iraq and Afghanistan reveal an increasing dependence by Western governments on private assistance. UN figures reveal that by 2007 there were up to 20,000 Afghan and 6,000 Western PMC operatives in Afghanistan.[20] The figures for Iraq are even higher – by 2008, nearly 200,000 PMC contractors were operating in the country, with around 30,000 of these providing an explicit security function, and the rest fulfilling other logistical or reconstruction tasks.[21] This figure outstripped the actual number of coalition troops serving in Iraq at that time, with private contractors constituting around 57 per cent of all in-theatre personnel.[22] Between 2003 and 2007, the US government spent $6–10 billion on contracts to PMCs for security-related work inside Iraq alone.[23] UN statistics suggest that the total global figure for PMC contracts awarded by states around the world since the 9/11 attacks up until 2007 could be as high as $100 billion – a vague figure given the complicated nature of contract awards and the accounting mechanisms of some PMCs.[24]

We must remember, however, that the use of contracted external fighters is a long-established trend in war, utilized by both the Ancient Greeks and the Roman Empire. Yet, despite more recent attempts to curtail the prevalence of mercenaries (such as the 1989 Convention Against the Recruitment, Use, Financing and Training of Mercenaries[25]), privatized military force remains legal because of the technical delineation between the proscribed individual profiteering of mercenaries and the permissible business functions of a registered company. In an effort to increase the oversight of PMCs at the international level, the United Nations established a Working Group on the Use of Mercenaries in 2005, a body of five experts who replaced the position of single rapporteur in place since 1987. The new body's mandate was expanded to cover PMCs as well as mercenaries, and particularly concerned itself with the impact PMCs were having on human rights. Jose Gomez del Prado, a member of the working group, argued publicly that the utilization of PMC contractors for paramilitary purposes was 'unlawful' and placed them on the same moral plain as terrorists.[26] Del Prado's assertion, although outspoken, raises the pertinent issue of PMC legitimacy and accountability in the realm of warfare. With the proliferation of PMCs and the subsequent marketization of security, modes of accountability for such actors are inevitably going to stem from the market in which they competitively operate. This is a far from sufficient mechanism because it leaves market forces as the primary bulwark against excessive force or illegal activity. If the market becomes the only real source of accountability for PMCs, then this rather intangibly leaves PMCs with only the vaguest sense of 'corporate-social responsibility' to act as a check on their actions. It also reflects the difficulties in attaining and enforcing international legal frameworks to monitor their activities, in addition to any voluntary codes of conduct that PMCs may enunciate. In short, the increased use of PMCs widens the democratic deficit in terms of the accountability of conduct in warfare (*jus in bello*) because actors outside the parameters of state or international control are becoming increasingly involved in more and more facets of warfare.

If the accountability of PMCs in Iraq is a future indicator of their role in future wars, then the implications are worrying. Contracts worth less than $25,000 were granted on an oral basis with no paperwork by the Coalition Provisional Authority (CPA), while any contract worth more than that was not required to be tendered on a competitive basis. Furthermore, the day before sovereignty was returned to the Iraqi interim government in June 2004, CPA chief Paul Bremer signed CPA Order #17, which bestowed immunity from prosecution to all PMC contractors in Iraq. The levels of accountability, from the nature of contract procurement to the conduct of PMC operatives on the ground, were negligible.[27] However, PMCs themselves have started to increase their professionalization mechanisms and accountability protocols. American PMCs are now bound by the Uniform Code of Military Justice and must now conform to a revised State Department 'Worldwide Personnel Protective Services' contract.[28] This represents a distinct effort on behalf of PMCs to ameliorate the reputation of recklessness that they have arguably attained during the wars in Afghanistan and Iraq in particular. Such conformity to the same regulations that bind the regular US military also paves the way for more 'legitimate' justification of their use by the US government in the future – especially in a proxy war context.

Peter Singer has posited that the growth in PMCs since the end of the Cold War has 'deprivileged' the state's security responsibilities.[29] However, this would be to imply that the state was reluctantly usurped of its monopoly of violence. Instead, states – predominantly Western ones – have willingly conceded this monopoly by co-opting PMCs into the security bargain. It is thus difficult to argue against Shawn Engbrecht's conclusion that PMCs are going to be 'integral to the future war-fighting machine' of the United States.[30] But the utilization of private military force is not exclusive to states, or indeed to the West. For example, in 1995, an alliance of Arab nations paid for a PMC to train the Bosnian army in order to assist in the protection of Bosnian Muslims and help counter the perceived influence of Iranian military aid coming into the country.[31] Non-state actors have also been recipients of PMC assistance. During the 1990s, an Israeli PMC, Hod Hahanit, was indicted for training Columbian paramilitaries who subsequently assassinated two leading politicians and bombed a civilian airplane.[32] It is also not beyond the realms of possibility that international organizations may need to resort to PMC usage in the future. Although the UN has hitherto been wary of the role played by PMCs in international security, it is not inconceivable that in the future stretched UN peacekeeping missions may be augmented by PMCs to fulfil certain functions. Such a hypothetical situation reveals to us the new ways in which the facets of contemporary security can impact upon the dynamics of proxy wars in the future. Another such facet is the potential significance of cyber warfare and its implications for use by proxy.

Cyber Warfare as a Mode of Proxy War

Although the utilization of PMCs may provide an arm's-length mode of proxy war fighting in the future, there are other mechanisms that disguise the proxy war-wagers' identities to a greater extent. Cyber warfare is a prime example of this. Playing upon our contemporary reliance on computer networks for our day-to-day existence, cyber warfare is an ideal vehicle for a proxy strategy given the difficulties in tracing the exact origin of cyber attacks. As a *New Scientist* article observed in December 2010, although 'no nation-state has ever been definitively linked to an act of cyber warfare . . . the internet is certainly being used as a battlefield'.[33] This relatively high degree of anonymity seemingly complements the long-established appeals of an indirect proxy war strategy. Add to this an understanding that computer technology is an easier and less obvious component to delegate to proxies than large quantities of weapons, cyber warfare adds an additional strand of plausible deniability to the undertaking of a cyber war by proxy. Large surrogate armies are no longer integral to the needs of a proxy war strategy. Developments in communications and information technology have to a large degree nullified the twentieth-century belief in 'boots on the ground' as a proxy war necessity. Computers can now create infrastructural damage to a foreign country of a kind that surrogate armies could not. The twenty-first century is thus likely to see more proxy wars fought by proxy servers than by proxy forces.

The Washington-based Center for Strategic and International Studies estimated that between May 2006 and June 2011 there had been at least seventy-eight 'significant cyber incidents' that had resulted in 'successful attacks on government agencies, defence and high tech companies, or economic crimes with losses of more than a million dollars'.[34] Included in these cyber attacks were repeated hacking attempts into the computer networks of the US State, Commerce and Defence departments; a massive service denial attack on the Estonian government network by suspected Russian hackers in May 2007; the hacking in April 2010 of classified files at the Indian Defence Ministry, reportedly by Chinese-based hackers, relating to Indian missile systems; and a cyber attack in January 2011, again by suspected Chinese hackers, that temporarily suspended usage by several Canadian government departments. Another recent example is a purportedly Chinese-sponsored scam in 2012 that involved setting up a fake Facebook page for NATO Supreme Allied Commander Europe, Admiral James Stavridis, in order to lure private information out of his close friends and family.[35] In June 2012, the Director of MI5, Jonathan Evans, made a rare public speech (his first in two years) to speak out against the 'industrial-scale processes involving many thousands of people lying behind both state-sponsored cyber espionage and organized cyber crime . . . The extent of what is going on is astonishing.'[36]

Perhaps the most significant example of a proxy war strategy already at work in the cyber realm was the 2012 revelation that the global Stuxnet virus was indeed a leaked computer worm designed by the Americans to covertly halt the enrichment of uranium at Iran's main nuclear facility in Nantanz. Originally conceived of under the Bush administration, but expanded by President Obama, the project to cripple Iranian nuclear facilities through cyber attacks – codenamed Olympic Games by security officials – was inadvertently made public in mid-2010 after a programming error in the virus launched it on to the World Wide Web. Cyber security experts, uncertain of its origins and intentions, labelled the virus Stuxnet, and watched helplessly as the virus spread. Despite this security breach, the White House authorized at least two further attacks on the Nananz plant by a refined version of the computer worm, which reports indicate knocked out 1,000 of the 5,000 uranium purification centrifuges in operation.[37] This was the first time that the US had engaged in large-scale cyber warfare by directing a cyber attack against the infrastructure of another country, causing the centrifuges to effectively self-destruct. Obama administration officials privately thought that the Iranian attack set Tehran's purported nuclear weapons attainment programme back around two years, although both the veracity of the programme's existence and the damage caused by Stuxnet are disputed.[38] Stuxnet was developed and executed by the US National Security Agency in conjunction with Unit 8200, a technical branch of the Israeli military. This close liaison was in part a deliberate attempt by the US to divert Israel away from direct military action in Iran over the nuclear issue, and maintain a covert, indirect strategy for keeping Iranian regional ambitions in check. This was to be a very modern indirect intervention: a benefactor in search of a proxy turning not to a third-party military unit but to a computer virus in order to undermine an enemy. It also revealed how the resort to a cyber attack against Iran's nuclear facilities – over which serious questions remain about their potential weapons-creation capabilities – possessed a lower element of risk than the other serious alternative uses of force, including air strikes.[39]

With examples like the Stuxnet attacks in mind, it is clear that states are now adapting to the new frontier of warfare that developments in cyberspace have opened up. Yet serious questions remain about whether cyber attacks constitute an egregious use of force, especially if these lead to civilian casualties (for example, as a result of a deliberate power outage at a hospital, or as a consequence of a plane crash caused by hacked air traffic control systems). So far, cyber attacks have tended to target critical infrastructures, and have been designed to undermine an enemy's financial or bureaucratic functioning. International statutes on the use of force are increasingly anachronistic as states increasingly utilize indirect methods of force, using computers not armies, 'botnets' not bombs.

Symptomatic of this was the move in May 2010 by the US Department of Defence to establish its own Cyber Command to coordinate offensive *and* defensive cyber network operations. Although often held responsible for the majority of global cyber attacks, China has itself been on the receiving end of many cyber attacks. The Chinese National Computer Network Emergency Response Co-ordination Centre reported that in 2010 China was the victim of 500,000 cyber attacks in that year alone.[40] Cyber warfare is thus a seemingly double-edged sword for China. Its rise as a global superpower, with all the attendant concerns about expanding its political and economic interests, holds a host of connotations for the question of the use of force and the potential utility of a widespread proxy war strategy.

The Rise of China and the Appeal of Proxy War

The rise of China as a global power has provoked profuse amounts of consternation and intrigue in the West as to how this communist state will reconcile its inherent inwardness with newfound inclinations towards international economic and political influence.[41] China's rise to superpower status has been one of stealth. New superpowers historically have emerged from the ashes of a large military conflict (such as the US after the Second World War) or aggressive periods of colonization (notably Britain in the nineteenth century). But China has avoided military confrontation with rival powers, thus breaking the mould of superpower establishment. Becoming a superpower is one thing, but remaining one is a different thing altogether. As China seeks to consolidate its new power status, the world's other superpowers look on with trepidation. In the early 1980s, Michael Doyle cautioned us against 'the single, greatest, traditional danger of international change – the transition between hegemonic leaders. When one great power begins to lose its pre-eminence and slip into mere equality, a warlike resolution of the international pecking order becomes exceptionally likely.'[42] There are currently huge economic and political pressures being placed on the liberal basis of American power by a global financial crisis and the legacies of two sapping and controversial wars in Iraq and Afghanistan. When combined with the rise of an illiberal China, those 'warlike resolutions' Doyle alludes to do not automatically have to be conventional, nuclear or large scale in their nature. Indeed, as this book has sought to demonstrate, they are more likely to be indirect resolutions and increasingly likely to involve some form of proxy, largely because of the high levels of economic interdependence the two countries have, which can be seen as a bulwark to the undertaking of other forms of direct confrontation.

There is no doubt that the rise of China as a global superpower is giving Washington reasons for concern, on both an economic and military front. Indeed, one of the most significant aspects of the important January 2012 US defence review was the overt strategic pivot towards the Asia-Pacific region, as priorities shifted to accommodate the rise of China: 'Over the long term, China's emergence as a regional power will have the potential to affect the US economy and our security in a variety of ways ... However, the growth of China's military power must be accompanied by greater clarity of its strategic intentions in order to avoid causing friction in the region.'[43] Washington's wariness over Chinese strategic intentions were compounded in March 2012 when Beijing announced an 11 per cent increase in its defence budget, topping $100 billion for the first ever time.[44] Yet it remains crucial to consider that China and the US are playing different games, with different rules. China is not seeking to establish a global military presence, or to impress its politico-economic creed on other states, as has been the foundation of American foreign policy since the Truman Doctrine. China's reliance on economic expansionism may avoid a Cold War-style superpower stand-off, but instead it raises a whole different prospect of a global power shift, as a result of China maximizing *indirect* uses of its power to secure long-term interests (both economic and political) while reducing the risk of war with the US.

China's rise has in large part been down to its profuse wielding of 'soft-power' mechanisms that have showcased their economic prowess above all else. Many of these efforts have focused upon underpinning the long-term future of their economic potency by securing resource access, trade agreements and, crucially, political influence in the developing world, especially Africa. Examples of Beijing's 'soft-power' projection include the funding of a 500 mile railway line from the iron ore mining region of Gabon to its main coastal port; the construction of a major highway between Entebbe and Kampala in Uganda; and the establishment of a Chinese university campus and hospital in Ghana.[45] This is in addition to the deployment of Chinese peacekeeping troops to Burundi, the Ivory Coast and Liberia, not to mention the billions of dollars-worth of loans to numerous African nations (secured against their natural resources). By 2008, China was conducting $108 billion-worth of trade with countries in Africa, up from only $10 billion eight years earlier.[46] A presence in the developing world is thus evidently integral to China's growth strategy.

The big question, however, remains how the rise of China will interact over the coming decades with the other trends identified in this chapter in relation to their effect on the proliferation of proxy wars. China's long-standing foreign policy 'golden rule' of non-interference in the internal affairs of other countries (arguably stemming from Mao Zedong's introspective view of communism, as opposed to Lenin's pursuit of global revolution) will be severely tested as the Chinese Communist Party (CCP) seeks ways to maintain high levels of economic growth with limited amounts of domestic natural resources and an expanding population. China's current access to African oil, cobalt, gold, copper and iron ore may well be constrained in the future by competitor states or internal disruption to supply (through civil war, for example). Two of the main catalysts to proxy wars identified in this book – interest and ideology – are compounded in the Chinese case, given the very nature of their one-party state. Furthermore, the issue of risk management is all the more acute in China's case due to the huge economic stakes involved in its new power status. The obsolescence of major war theory forwarded by John Mueller over twenty years ago arguably still holds true in the case of modern China. An assertive naval presence in the South China Sea, ongoing tensions over Taiwan, and President Obama's Asia 'pivot' strategy have all increased the bellicose rhetoric emanating from, and aimed at, China. However, the interdependence of the Chinese and American economies, combined with the overarching shadow that nuclear weapons continue to cast over international relations, arguably diminishes the chances of conventional war with China. Talk of China's peaceful rise to the status of global superpower needs to be heavily couched in terms that closely scrutinize China's *indirect* forms of power projection and interest maximization. Indeed, it could be argued that a form of proxy warfare has been simmering between China and the US for some time now, with the Americans using Taiwan as a regional surrogate to block expansions of Chinese military power. This allows us to see President Obama's authorization of a $6 billion arms deal with Taiwan in 2010 as an act of preventive proxy war, designed as a bulwark against Chinese regional enlargement.[47]

This, however, would not be the first time that perceptions of Chinese power have increased the appeal of proxy wars to their potential adversaries. Neil MacFarlane has argued that Nikita Khrushchev's adoption of an overt proxy war strategy in the Third World in the early 1960s was in part motivated 'by the emergence of China as a serious rival for influence among "progressive" forces in Africa and Asia'.[48] Such competition for influence, MacFarlane observes, may actually have accentuated the interventionist tendencies of the Kremlin to a degree they might otherwise have avoided. The Sino–Soviet split in the 1970s further enlarged the scope, and indeed the perceived need, for Soviet advancement in strategically sensitive areas.

Twenty-first-century Chinese influence in the developing world has in part rested upon its non-Western credentials. When assessed alongside Western-led initiatives, particularly by the International Monetary Fund (IMF), to introduce development initiatives, the Chinese model seemingly holds an appeal to certain African leaders given the absence of accountability and privatization stipulations attached to loans or investments. This has helped build economic and diplomatic ties between China and some African nations. Symptomatic of these bonds was the creation of initiatives such as the Forum on China-Africa Co-operation. But these bonds have yet to be truly tested, either through demands for support during a conflict or through pressures on vital resource access. The scope for Chinese engagement in proxy wars in Africa, although seemingly antithetical to their long-standing foreign policy doctrine, may soon increase as they seek ways of preserving their newfound wealth and status.[49] Additional considerations, such as China's desire to enhance its own energy security via African oil exports, the seeking of new investment opportunities on the continent, and the creation of new strategic alliances, will all play a role in how China responds to the security situation in Africa over the coming decades.[50]

The foundations of proxy intervention are arguably already being laid on the African continent. Not only has China posted fourteen defence attachés in embassies throughout Africa, but it also deployed 4,500 military personnel to Nigeria in 2007 to protect the important oil infrastructure and Chinese oil workers in the Niger Delta area from insurgent attack.[51] This latter example is intriguing for several reasons. First, it demonstrates a de facto Chinese proxy war taking place against an African non-state actor. Second, it reveals the vast extent of the Chinese presence in Africa. When taking into consideration the fact that all business contracts drawn up by Beijing require at least 70 per cent of the industrial labour force to be Chinese, there are now more Chinese in Nigeria than there were British colonial administrators at the height of London's imperial rule.[52] This has caused significant resentment, not just in Nigeria, but in other African countries too where a high influx of Chinese labour has squeezed out locals from the employment market and given rise to politicized accusations of neo-imperialism. Michael Sata, a candidate in Zambia's 2006 presidential election, argued during his campaign that 'the Chinese are not here as investors, they are here as invaders'.[53]

China's economic power, as its heavy investment in Africa demonstrates, is significant. But its adaptability to satisfy economic imperatives is only part of the discussion about how China is changing in the face of new challenges and opportunities on the global stage. China's evolution in terms of how its military perceives threats and attempts to secure strategic advantages is hugely significant too. In this regard, an important new document emerged from the Chinese military in early 1999 that is worth discussing. Written by two People's Liberation Army (PLA) colonels from the younger generation of the Chinese officer class, Qiao Liang and Wang Xiangsui, 'Unrestricted Warfare' advocated that China re-evaluate its very conceptualization of what war actually is in the wake of the 1990s 'Revolution in Military Affairs' (RMA) and wider changes to world politics, society and technology rendered by globalization. It is worth quoting at length in order to fully glean an understanding of their interpretation of future conflict:

> War which has undergone the changes of modern technol-
> ogy and the market system will be launched even more in
> atypical forms. In other words, whilst we are seeing a relative
> reduction in military violence, at the same time we definitely
> are seeing an increase in political, economic and techno-
> logical violence . . . When we suddenly realize that all these
> non-war actions may be the new factors constituting future
> warfare, we have to come up with a new name for this new
> form of war: Warfare which transcends all boundaries and
> limits, in short: unrestricted warfare. If this name becomes
> established . . . it means that all the boundaries lying
> between the two worlds of war and non-war, of military and
> non-military, will be totally destroyed, and it also means that
> many of the current principles of combat will be modified,
> and even that the rules of war may need to be re-written.[54]

'Unrestricted Warfare' made a dent in PLA thinking on the strategic outlook for the century ahead. The implications of this are crucial as its rationale as a mode of thinking for the PLA paves the way for an unlimited application of proxy war by China. Acknowledging the breakdown in traditional defini-tions of states of war and peace, Liang and Xiansui endorse the furthering of strategic objectives in increasingly indirect ways, including making use of cyberspace. 'Unrestricted Warfare' is an important document when evaluating how Chinese military thought is developing in line with changes to broader trends in international relations, especially increases in China's own power and influence. It represents a bold manifesto for limitless ways of conceiving the defeat of ene-mies. This, therefore, places the resort to proxy war at the heart of potential future options the Chinese may take up. If the number of alleged China-based cyber attacks is anything to go by, China's new era of unrestricted warfare may have already begun.

Conclusion
The Continuing Appeal of Proxy Warfare

This book represents an effort to reclaim the concept of proxy war away from its traditional Cold War connotations regarding superpower interference, and to redefine its parameters as a perennial component of warfare with renewed relevance to the direction of war in the modern world. If life is nasty, brutish and short, as Thomas Hobbes would have us believe, then it would appear that it is also imbued with a perpetual desire to interfere in the affairs of others. As K. J. Holsti has put it, 'intervention of one kind or other has become the norm' in international relations.[1] Proxy wars have thus retained an essential appeal to states despite the ending of the Cold War, the beginning (and seeming end) of a global War on Terror, and the rise and fall of different competitor superpower states.

Proxy warfare is a regular feature of modern conflict, yet it retains a high level of conceptual anonymity. Such conflicts are being currently fought in the world today and are often wrapped up in wider wars. This study has been an effort in highlighting the features of proxy wars in order to encourage a wider understanding of the causes, conduct and consequences of this commonly recurring but low-profile form of conflict. This is an endeavour undertaken with full acceptance of the relative anonymity of the label 'proxy war' in the scholarly literature on security, in media reports from war zones and, importantly, in the foreign policy and security declarations of policymakers themselves (in large part because they are often trying to keep any indirect intervention a secret). Let us take a recent high-profile conflict – the uprising in Syria that began in March 2011 – and explore how an underlying proxy war component has appealed to some of the warring factions without such a dynamic being given serious analytical exposure.

The intensification of President Bashar al-Assad's crackdown on dissident groups opposed to his nepotistic grip on power in early 2012 turned the world's gaze upon what appeared to be the latest instalment of the Arab Spring uprisings. Massacres of civilians in the towns of Homs and Houla prompted intense debate about the necessity and viability of launching a direct military intervention, potentially under the auspices of the United Nations, to put a stop to the atrocities. But there remained a distinct undertone to the discussions and requests of some of the parties involved in the violence that revealed a desire to turn the conflict in Syria into a war by proxy. At a February 2012 Arab League-sponsored 'Friends of Syria' conference in Tunisia, the anti-Assad Syrian National Council (SNC) lobbied the delegates of the seventy nations present to allow them to import weapons, in order for them to take their fight to the Syrian army and pro-government militias. As an SNC spokesperson stated: 'If the regime fails to . . . end violence against citizens, the Friends of Syria should not constrain individual countries from aiding the Syrian opposition by means of military advisers, training and provision of arms to defend themselves.'[2] This request was tantamount to a plea to the international community to intervene in Syria by proxy in an effort to undermine, and ultimately dislodge, President Assad from power. Yet this effort drew heavy criticism from some world leaders. Iraqi Prime Minister Nouri al-Maliki drew on his own country's recent experiences of proxy intervention to caution that 'the option to arm either side of the conflict will lead to a regional and international proxy war in Syria'.[3]

Despite al-Maliki's warning, it would appear that both friends and enemies of Assad's regime resorted to indirect intervention in Syria as a stalemate at the UN Security Council protracted the possibility of direct intervention. In March 2012, the British government announced it was doubling the non-military assistance budget to Syrian opposition groups to £500,000. Foreign Secretary William Hague indicated that the aid would cover communications equipment and civil society initiatives.[4] In questioning by the Senate Armed Services Committee in the same month, US Defence Secretary Leon Panetta refused to rule out supplying rebel groups with equipment in the future.[5] By August 2012, the British government had sanctioned a further £5 million-worth of 'non-lethal equipment' to anti-Assad groups inside Syria.[6] Allies of President Assad, namely Russia, have also been developing proxy methods by which to bolster their ally. Despite Kremlin denials that it was aiding Assad's crackdown against his own people, it was revealed in June 2012 that Russia was attempting to export attack helicopters and missiles to Assad after a Syrian-bound Russian cargo vessel, the MV *Alaed*, was halted off the coast of Scotland after its contents were revealed to the ship's London-based insurance company.[7] Speculation surrounding Russian proxy aid to Assad intensified in October 2012, when the Turkish military forced a Damascus-bound Russian passenger plane to land on suspicion it was being used to smuggle military equipment into Syria from Moscow.[8] On all sides of this increasingly internecine conflict, it seems that respective allies are resorting to proxy intervention as a means of assisting their cause from a distance in the face of international disagreement over the acceptability of direct intervention. The conflict in Syria, when seen alongside the proxy component of the intervention in Libya, marks out the ways in which the Arab Spring is potentially being turned into a giant proxy war, as Nouri al-Maliki feared. This stands as a testament to this form of war's continuing appeal to states who seek to maximize their own interest and/or ideological vision. Whether we are looking at examples from the Cold War, the War on Terror, or the Arab Spring, we can observe perpetual efforts on behalf of states and non-state actors to engage in forms of indirect war-waging.

Proxy Wars as 'the Cheapest Insurance in the World'

During the Cold War, the US utilized what they called 'foreign assistance programs' as their tool for waging proxy wars through indirect financial or materiel support for Third World allies engaged in either intra- or inter-state wars with communist opponents. At a National Security Council meeting, in late 1955, President Dwight Eisenhower described these proxy war programmes as 'the cheapest insurance in the world'.[9] Eisenhower appreciated exactly the ways in which proxy wars both reduce the financial burden and the political costs of outright military intervention. This logic asks the base question: why risk the lives of your own soldiers and purge your own treasury when you can get others to achieve the desired conflict outcome for you? The appeal of proxy strategies to policymakers, both then and now, comes couched in the perceived benefits of lower risk (no combat deaths, thus reduced political backlash) and plausible deniability (the symbolism of no direct intervention ensures no overt strategic defeat if the war is lost, but continued influence and enhanced interest if the war is won).

On top of the multiple international and domestic factors that motivate states to intervene in a conflict, whether overtly or covertly, the decision to do so is often heavily couched in interpretations of eventual success. By their very nature, superpowers engage in proxy wars because they wish to successfully influence the outcome of an existing conflict in their favour, yet they do not wish to fully commit to deploying their own troops. But insurance policies do not always pay out. For this reason, states have to be accepting of failure during proxy interventions, given the reluctance to send in their own military force in the first place. Much of what is called the 'kinetic' element of the conflict (essentially the actual war-fighting itself) is not done by the benefactor state; thus they have to vicariously rely on their proxies to achieve strategic victory for them. The defeat of a proxy client, such as occurred with many of the Soviet Union's Arab proxies during the Cold War, for example, was reluctantly accepted in the absence of a desire by the Kremlin to aid them without sending in Soviet ground forces. Yet, when looking at Soviet proxies across Africa and Asia, it can be argued, as Bruce Porter has done, that 'Soviet involvement [by proxy] in local conflicts has been highly successful . . . [which] must be attributed largely to its capacity to deliver arms rapidly and in the amounts necessary to fulfil the battlefield requirements of its clients'.[10] However, there is not always a correlation between short-term proxy war *success* and long-term benefactor *influence* over the client state or group. It has been discussed how Hizballah, for example, has outgrown its initial deference to Syria. Furthermore, consider how Iran may have engendered a hastened British withdrawal from southern Iraq via the adoption of a proxy war strategy, but the Sunni control over Iraqi politics remains in place, nullifying Iranian influence.

The Changing Dynamics of Proxy Wars

The undertaking of proxy wars by states, especially superpowers, is inextricably linked with their wider geostrategic concerns, prompted in the main by interest and ideology. Celeste Wallander argued in the late 1980s that 'all Soviet

military analysis of third world conflict is essentially derivative of ... their primary focus on general war, operations in
the European theatre, and the relation between conventional
and nuclear warfare'.[11] If we contemporize this observation to
reflect early twenty-first-century geostrategic debates it can be
argued that American military analysis of the global South is
essentially derivative of their primary focus on general war (a
result of their scarring experiences reacquainting themselves
with counter-insurgency warfare in Afghanistan and Iraq),
operations in the Asian theatre (a result of the rise of China
as a superpower competitor), and the relation between conventional and unconventional war (a result of intra-military
debates about the location of asymmetric warfare in US military doctrine and the prominence of potential 'hybrid wars'
that combine the two conflict types[12]). This analysis indeed
opens the door for more, rather than less, proxy wars in the
future given the continuation of proxy wars' core appeal even
in a changing strategic environment.

Modern-day proxy wars have become, in military parlance,
arm's-length 'effects-based operations', whereby a specific
objective is desired (such as the downfall of an authoritarian
regime) with the avoidance of a foreseen consequence (conflict escalation with a rival superpower, for example) and at
an acceptable monetary cost (an increasingly important factor
given the state of the contemporary global economy) – all of
which is achieved without a state having to directly commit
military forces of their own.

Since the Cold War ended superpower-induced proxy wars
have largely been replaced by proxy wars driven by regional
powers via the cross-border percolation of militia groups.
Such proxy wars, witnessed especially in Africa, have seen
their character shift from internationalized conflicts of an
ideological nature to regionalized interventions motivated by
inter- and intra-state competition for power and resources. As

Jon Abbink has argued in relation to the African case: 'The nature and extent of proxy wars need to be studied more systematically because they have a serious impact on long-term stability and regional peace in Africa and reveal patterns of international and regional African power politics that often get neglected.'[13]

Another revealing trend is the increasingly multilateral way in which proxy wars are being waged. The predominantly unilateral way in which the two Cold War superpowers provided their chosen proxies with arms, training and money has become transplanted in the early twenty-first century with coalition proxy warfare. That is not to say that single-state proxy strategies are obsolete, as they will of course continue, but merely that there has been a trend towards collective proxy strategies. This has taken the form of either deliberate proxy coalitions, such as certain NATO countries collectively harnessing indirect means of support for anti-Gaddafi forces during the 2011 Libya uprising, or of informal alliances that stem from mutual selection of the same proxy, such as that which united Syria and Iran through their support for Hizballah in their battle against the Israeli state. There is thus a knock-on effect on understandings of how collective security is perceived within contemporary international relations. The decision by groups of states to intervene by proxy in an existing conflict reveals not only a shared interest in the outcome of that war, but also demonstrates how collective security – through the removal of a mutually despised regime, for example – is not necessarily manifest through formal treaties and alliance making, but is something that is being more informally undertaken by the aiding and assisting of allies from a distance. Joint missile shields or collective security clauses in alliance pacts can now be joined by coalition proxy war-fighting as a manifestation of collective security in action in the twenty-first century.

Our understanding of what indeed constitutes a 'proxy' has also been challenged by certain non-state actors in recent years. Insurgent groups in Iraq and Irish republican splinter groups have pioneered the use of what could be labelled 'unwilling tactical proxies' by forcibly using individuals against their will to undertake acts of terrorism. This book is replete with examples of what is arguably a 'classical' understanding of a proxy war – states utilizing compliant non-state surrogates to fulfil strategic objectives (such as the downfall of an enemy government or defeat of a rival military force). But the near monopoly of large-scale *strategic* objectives fulfilled by *armies* or organizations acting as proxies, has been undermined by the recourse on the part of some groups to the utilization of *individuals* to fulfil *tactical* acts of violence in a forceful manner. Two high-profile examples spring to mind. In 2005, it was widely reported how a militia group in Iraq had coercively induced a man with Down's Syndrome to undertake a suicide attack on their behalf against a polling station in order to disrupt American-backed elections in the country.[14] Five years later, it was revealed that in order to have a car bomb explode outside of a British army barracks in Northern Ireland, dissident republicans opposed to the power-sharing Good Friday Agreement hijacked a taxi in Belfast, held the taxi driver's family hostage, and promised to release them only once the driver had delivered the bomb in his cab to the barracks.[15] In both of these examples coercive force was used by the groups to ensure that tactical-level acts of violence were undertaken – but by using individuals to act as the proxy. It is becoming evident that acts of proxy war now percolate all levels of warfare, from the geostrategic objective down to the lone act of violence.

Another interesting contemporary element of the changing nature of proxies to consider is the jihadist interpretation of their role in their perceived 'holy struggle'. Members of al-Qaeda and other affiliated groups see themselves as doing God's work on earth, defeating the enemies of Islam. In effect, they see themselves as proxy clients of God. This is important because it changes the dimension of causation of proxy conflict when the 'benefactor' is not a state but a deity. The strategic objectives of a state have in some cases been replaced by adherences to fulfil the particular interpretations of a religious text. But unlike the ideologically informed proxy wars of the Cold War era, this religiously inspired proxy war against the West on behalf of al-Qaeda (which was arguably codified by Osama bin Laden in his 1998 'declaration of war'[16]) is one that is not necessarily held to the same standards or strategic rationale of leaders operating in the state system because of the perpetuity of the jihadist interpretation of their struggle. In short, they will act as proxies on earth for God until the struggle is won. Seeing al-Qaeda's war against the West through the lens of proxy war, and not necessarily counter-terrorism or counter-insurgency, places a new spin on our understanding of the causes and consequences of waging a War on Terror (most importantly because it undermines the notion that Islamist fundamentalism can be defeated outright, so long as its adherents see themselves as momentary proxies of God locked in an eternal holy war).

The Consequences of Proxy Wars

The proxy wars explored in this book reveal a threefold set of consequences for those involved, including benefactors, proxies, surrogates and the population of the country where the intervention is taking place. The consequences are not necessarily immediate and are often protracted in their impact. In short, proxy wars can detrimentally induce: dependence in the long run between the benefactor and the proxy (politically and financially); an elongation and/or intensification of the original war in which intervention was sought; and the creation of either conflict overspill beyond the initial boundaries of the war or unintended 'blowback' for the participants once the war has ended.

Dependence
The National Liberation movements that were on the receiving end of so much Soviet assistance in their fight against pro-Western or colonial governments during the Cold War were acting, according to Neil MacFarlane, to achieve four overriding objectives: political independence; freedom from external economic control; social revolution; and cultural regeneration.[17] The USSR was intent on fostering such close ties with these groups that assistance arguably bred dependence. To the same extent, the upshot of widespread covert American proxy interventions during the Cold War, especially in Africa, to undermine this dependence of Soviet aid led, as Stephen Weissman pointed out in the late 1970s, to 'increasing dependence by the moderates on US and CIA support and growing popular anti-Americanism'.[18]

In the bipolar atmosphere of Cold War tensions, the imposed political and economic dependence of colonial rule against which so many guerrilla groups were fighting was transposed for a similar dependence on superpower patronage to provide political stability, ideological guidance and economic aid in a postcolonial setting. These are the ties that seemingly still bind state benefactors and their non-state proxies today. Benefactor states are still looked to in order to provide ongoing support across the political, economic and military spectrum.

Prolonged and/or intensified violence
There is often an assumption that the adoption of a proxy war strategy is the quickest way to bring a war to a swift end, by

indirectly allowing one side to gain an advantage in terms of manpower, training or weaponry. This notion was advocated most recently by President George W. Bush's former envoy to Sudan, Andrew S. Natsios, who argued that the conflict between the newly independent South Sudan and its northerly neighbour Sudan could be brought to a halt if America indirectly intervened in favour of its South Sudanese allies in the face of Northern aggression:

> To stop the killing the international community must arm South Sudan. Unlike intervention in Afghanistan and Iraq, the United States need not fire any shots. Just as we have provided weapons to support Israel but never put our own troops at risk, we can help bring peace to this region . . . The only way to end the North's bullying and foster peace talks is to give the South the right tools: American anti-aircraft weapons.[19]

But the understanding that proxy interventions actually prematurely *end* an existing conflict belies evidence that on the whole they actually *prolong* such conflicts, largely because a weak warring faction is boosted to the point of creating stalemate. Indeed, in June 2012, an Amnesty International report into the situation in South Sudan chronicled how both Sudan and South Sudan had sought proxy assistance in efforts to undermine each other, including Chinese-made landmines and Ukrainian tanks. Such assistance, the report concluded, had helped contribute to 'serious human rights abuses and violations of international humanitarian law'.[20]

But conflict elongation and intensification as a result of proxy intervention is not new. As Stanley Payne has argued in relation to the Kremlin-backed International Brigades sent to fight in Spain during their civil war: 'Soviet intervention managed to block the victory of the right, but its dimensions were not great enough to achieve the victory of the left. It was adequate only to guarantee a more prolonged civil war.'[21] Hugh

Thomas was in agreement, citing proxy interventions as 'one reason why the war lasted so long'.[22] Such examples highlight how a flood of weapons or surrogate forces into an existing war zone gives one or other of the parties involved further motivation and support to fight on, rather than collapse or seek negotiation.

Overspill and 'blowback'

To a large degree, the arming or training of proxies by benefactor states is based on the geostrategic assumption that 'my enemy's enemy is my friend'. Yet, as the history of proxy war tells us, this policy runs the severe risk of creating unintended, counterproductive consequences once the war is over – what the CIA terms 'blowback'. Such blowback can be high profile or subtle, immediate or delayed in its manifestation.[23] The future consequences of foreign policy decisions are arguably exacerbated in proxy war situations given the often fleeting nature of the relationship between the benefactor and the proxy, and the typically short-term nature of the benefactor's strategic objective. This leaves the long-term consequences of the intervention unpondered. The proliferation of proxy wars during the Cold War era intensified the frequency and effect of blowback. As Chalmers Johnson concluded in *Blowback,* his provocative study of the implications of recent US foreign policy: 'world politics in the twenty-first century will in all likelihood be driven primarily by blowback from the second half of the twentieth century – that is, from the unintended consequences of the Cold War and the crucial American decision to maintain a Cold War posture in a post-Cold War world'.[24] Johnson's cautionary assessment should encourage us to not only reflect more deeply on the contemporary consequences of proxy wars waged in the past, but also make policymakers and scholars alike more vigilant as to the potential long-term implications of initiating short-term proxy wars today.

Perhaps the exemplary manifestation of blowback is how the Stinger missiles provided by the US to the Afghan mujahedeen during the late 1980s were used in conflicts much further afield after the Soviets withdrew in 1989. The use of Stinger missiles by non-state actors with whom no direct Stinger sales have been made, but who had interaction with Afghan groups who were supplied with American Stingers, has been reported in Bosnia, Iran, Kashmir, Tunisia and the Palestinian territories in the years since the Soviet withdrawal.[25] Indeed, so concerned did Washington become at the proliferation of Stinger usage that President George H. W. Bush authorized a $65 million 'buy back' programme to help the CIA retrieve as many of the missiles as possible. The results of this initiative were negligible, with only a small fraction of the Stingers recovered, leaving somewhere between 300 and 600 unaccounted for.[26] The effects of this particular proxy war decision long outlasted both the original conflict it was designed to influence and unwittingly spilled over the borders of the country they were intended for.

The Soviet–Afghan War killed 1.3 million people, with 5.5 million more turned into refugees – a third of the nation's pre-war population.[27] The end of this conflict coincided with the sudden and unexpected end to the entire Cold War, causing, in the words of the 9/11 Commission Report, a 'trauma in the foreign policy and national security community both in and out of government'.[28] This policy malaise was perfectly encapsulated by the way in which the US attempted to extract itself from this particular proxy war. The jihadist diaspora that was created at the end of the Afghan war ignited a new wave of pan-Arab fundamentalism. By walking away from the mujahedeen groups after the Cold War, the US was complicit in creating a transnational force of Islamist militants who went on to establish terrorist movements around the world, and indeed for permitting Afghanistan to slide into civil war and doing little to alleviate Afghanistan's poverty levels, which were amongst the highest in the world. In addition to the civil war and continuing poverty, one of the most significant consequences of US inattention to Afghanistan after 1989 was the sanctuary now on offer to an international array of jihadist militants. By the mid-1990s the Taliban had won control of large swathes of the country, including the capital Kabul. As a result, Afghanistan was established as a safe haven for Islamic fundamentalism, compounded by the fact that the US had no clear policy formulated to deal with the issue. The Americans had given little thought to the repercussions of their proxy war strategy. When Zbigniew Brzezinski, President Carter's National Security Advisor, was pressed on this issue in a 1998 interview with a French news magazine, he retorted: 'Which was more important in world history? The Taliban or the fall of the Soviet Empire? A few over-excited Islamists or the liberation of Central Europe and the end of the Cold War?'[29] Although the Americans may have helped end one war, they unwittingly sowed the seeds for the start of another one, which was made startlingly clear on 11 September 2001.[30] As easy as it may be to apportion this blame, it must be acknowledged that America 'was doing what great powers have done throughout history, in order to survive as great powers: pursue its strategic interests'.[31] Such strategic interests, this book has aimed to demonstrate, are often pursued indirectly, frequently in secret, inevitably for reasons of power and/or ideology, and by using the personnel of other states or non-state actors to vicariously fulfil those interests for them.

Proxy Wars in the Modern World

Proxy warfare is a type of conflict seemingly full of paradoxes. It is neither full intervention nor non-intervention; it can be either overt or covert; it can be utilized by states and non-state actors, sometimes against one another. This book has been an effort in clarifying some of these seeming contradictions. It has also attempted to highlight not just the perpetual recourse to proxy intervention in the history of warfare, but also to signpost ways in which it is going to become a prominent part of future conflict. Proxy wars are not merely relics of Cold War superpower competition. Indeed, they are likely to be an increasingly used facet in the rivalry between today's existing and rising superpowers. As such, proxy wars need to be understood more thoroughly by students, scholars and policymakers alike if their more damaging consequences are to be avoided in the decades to come.

An understanding of proxy wars as the indirect engagement in a conflict by third parties wishing to influence its strategic outcome helps bring clarity to opaque discussions, or when reporting on conflicts around the world in which the hidden hand of a benefactor is vicariously assisting a chosen party. Proxy wars have been far more prominent in the past and present of warfare than the academic literature, policy debates or journalism has acknowledged. In part, this is because of the perpetual greyness of proxy war definitions and the often secret nature of proxy war-waging. It is high time some colour was brought to such definitional debates, and a light shone on the motives, methods and identities of those who have sought to interfere in existing conflicts while attempting to keep their hands clean.

Some elements of proxy wars have remained constant throughout the decades. Foremost among these are the reasons for their appeal and why states engage in them. The alluring combination of plausible deniability and lower risk has ensured that proxy wars offer an attraction to states seeking to defend or expand their interests or ideology. This allure, however, brings with it inherent dangers that must remain under heavy scrutiny as a new era of proxy wars inevitably beckons. Whether these proxy interventions are undertaken between the US and China in Africa, or by anonymous states in cyberspace, or by PMCs in the developing world, indirect interference in existing conflicts may reduce conflict escalation, but risk conflict intensification. They may circumvent the potential international political uproar at a direct intervention, but they increase the chances of higher casualties as a result of the influx of externally sourced weapons, money or personnel. In short, the history of proxy wars needs closer inspection if their manifestation in the foreseeable future is to be appropriately understood, adequately contextualized and sufficiently critiqued. The onus is on us to ensure that is the case.

Notes

INTRODUCTION: THE RISE OF PROXY WARS

1 The two recent exceptions to this are Geraint Hughes, *My Enemy's Enemy: Proxy Warfare in International Politics* (Brighton: Sussex Academic Press, 2012), and Michael Innes (ed.), *Making Sense of Proxy Wars: States, Surrogates and the Use of Force* (Dulles, VA: Potomac Books, 2012).

2 K. J. Holsti, *The State, War and the State of War* (Cambridge: Cambridge University Press, 1996), p. xi.

3 For example, see Richard Ned Lebow, *Why Nations Fight* (Cambridge: Cambridge University Press, 2010); John Vasquez, *The War Puzzle Revisited* (Cambridge: Cambridge University Press, 2009); and Geoffrey Blainey, *The Causes of War* (London: Macmillan, 1973).

4 Odd Arne Westad, *The Global Cold War: Third World Interventions and the Making of Our Times* (Cambridge: Cambridge University Press, 2007).

5 For example, see Nicholas Wheeler, *Saving Strangers: Humanitarian Intervention in International Society* (Oxford: Oxford University Press, 2000) and Alex Bellamy, *Responsibility to Protect* (Cambridge: Polity, 2009).

6 John Mueller, *Retreat from Doomsday: The Obsolescence of Major War* (New York: Basic Books, 1989).

7 Andrew Mumford, 'Counter-Insurgency Research: A Case of Recurring Amnesia', *International Studies Today* 1/1(2011): 1–2.

8 Joseph Stiglitz and Linda Bilmes, *The Three Trillion Dollar War: The True Cost of the Iraq Conflict* (London: Penguin, 2009).

CHAPTER 1 WHAT IS PROXY WAR?

1 Chris Loveman, 'Assessing the Phenomenon of Proxy Intervention', *Conflict, Security and Development* 2/3(2002): 30.
2 For a comprehensive study of this proxy war, see Amanda Foreman, *A World on Fire: An Epic History of Two Nations Divided* (London: Penguin, 2011).
3 Philip Towle, 'The Strategy of War by Proxy', *RUSI Journal* 126/1(1981): 21.
4 Harold Tillema, 'Foreign Overt Military Intervention in the Nuclear Age', *Journal of Peace Research* 26/2(1989): 179.
5 Karl W. Deutsch, 'External Involvement in Internal Wars', in Harry Eckstein (ed.), *Internal War: Problems and Approaches* (New York: Free Press of Glencoe, 1964), p. 102.
6 Richard Ned Lebow, *Why Nations Fight* (Cambridge: Cambridge University Press, 2010), p. 97.
7 K. J. Holsti, *The State, War and the State of War* (Cambridge: Cambridge University Press, 1996), p. 22.
8 Hedley Bull, *Intervention in World Politics* (Oxford: Oxford University Press, 1984), p. 181.
9 Yaacov Bar-Siman-Tov, 'The Strategy of War by Proxy', *Cooperation and Conflict* 19(1984): 263–73.
10 Ibid., p. 264.
11 Bertil Dunér, 'Proxy Intervention in Civil Wars', *Journal of Peace Research* 18/4(1981): 353–61.
12 Loveman, 'Assessing the Phenomenon of Proxy Intervention', p. 31.
13 Bruce D. Porter, *The USSR in Third World Conflicts: Soviet Arms and Diplomacy in Local Wars, 1945–80* (Cambridge: Cambridge University Press, 1984), p. 220.
14 Alastair Smith, 'To Intervene or Not to Intervene: A Biased Decision', *Journal of Conflict Resolution* 40/1(1996): 34.
15 Morton Halperin, *Limited War in the Nuclear Age* (New York: John Wiley & Sons, 1963), pp. 3–25.
16 Lawrence Freedman, *Kennedy's Wars: Berlin, Cuba, Laos and Vietnam* (New York: Oxford University Press, 2002), p.xii.
17 Stanley Karnow, *Vietnam: A History* (London: Penguin, 1997), p. 268.
18 Hans Morgenthau, 'To Intervene or Not to Intervene', *Foreign Affairs* 45/3(1967): 425 and 428.

19 Patrick M. Regan, *Civil Wars and Foreign Powers: Outside Intervention in Intrastate Conflict* (Ann Arbor, MI: University of Michigan Press, 2002), p. 10.

20 Ibid, p. 11.

21 For a thorough analysis of the use of drones as part of America's 'war on terror', see Brian Glyn Williams, 'The CIA's Covert Predator Drone Strikes in Pakistan, 2004-2010: The History of an Assassination Campaign', *Studies in Conflict and Terrorism* 33/10(2010): 871–92.

22 Interview with Leon Panetta, 'Obama's Middle East Strategy', *New Perspectives Quarterly* 26/3(2009): 38.

23 Jo Becker and Scott Shane, 'Secret "Kill List" Proves a Test of Obama's Principles and Will', *The New York Times*, 29 May 2012; available at: <http://www.nytimes.com/2012/05/29/world/obamas-leadership-in-war-on-al-qaeda.html?pagewanted=all>.

24 Ibid.

25 P. W. Singer, *Wired for War: The Robotics Revolution and Conflict in the Twenty-First Century* (New York: Penguin, 2010), p. 33.

26 Ibid., p. 37.

27 CIA, *Consumer's Guide to Intelligence* (Washington, DC, 1995), quoted in David F. Rudgers, 'The Origins of Covert Action', *Journal of Contemporary History* 35/2(2003): 249.

28 This differs from Geraint Hughes' recent argument that proxy wars are 'a military/paramilitary aspect of covert action.' *My Enemy's Enemy: Proxy Warfare in International Politics* (Brighton: Sussex Academic Press, 2012), p. 5.

29 Quoted in Rudgers, 'The Origins of Covert Action', p. 249.

30 For a thorough deconstruction of the theory and practice of covert action by the US since 1945, see Gregory F. Treverton, *Covert Action: The Limits of Intervention in the Postwar World* (New York: Basic Books, 1987) – although, crucially (and erroneously), Treverton folds up the essential characteristics of proxy wars and places them under the covert action banner.

31 Robert Fisk, 'America's Secret Plan to Arm Libya's Rebels', *The Independent*, 7 March 2011, available at: <http://www.independent.co.uk/news/world/middle-east/americas-secret-plan-to-arm-libyas-rebels-2234227.html>.

32 BBC News online, 'Obama Not Ruling Out Arming Libya Rebels', 30 March 2011, at <http://www.bbc.co.uk/news/world-africa-12902450?print=true>.

33 Xan Rice, Ian Traynor and Ian Black, 'Libyan Rebels Loaned
    £800 Million in Fight to Force Gaddafi's Departure', *Guardian*, 9
    June 2011, available at: <http://www.guardian.co.uk/world/2011/
    jun/09/libyan-rebels-foreign-goverment-loans?CMP=twt_fd>.
34 Towle, 'The Strategy of War by Proxy', p. 22.
35 Antony Beevor, *The Battle for Spain: The Spanish Civil War, 1936–
    1939* (New York: Penguin, 2006), p. 187.
36 Towle, 'The Strategy of War by Proxy', p. 22.
37 Beevor, *The Battle for Spain*, p. 139.
38 Hugh Thomas, *The Spanish Civil War*, 4th edn (London: Penguin,
    2003), p. 432.
39 Ibid., p. 438.
40 Gerald Howson, *Arms for Spain: The Untold Story of the Spanish
    Civil War* (London: John Murray, 1998), pp. 278–303.
41 Beevor, *The Battle for Spain*, p. 157.
42 Thomas, *The Spanish Civil War*, p. 440.
43 Ibid., pp. 913–14.
44 Ibid., p. 455.
45 Ibid., p.556.

CHAPTER 2 WHY DOES PROXY WAR APPEAL?

1 Frederic S. Pearson, 'Foreign Military Interventions and
   Domestic Disputes', *International Studies Quarterly* 18/3(1974):
   262.
2 Stanley G. Payne, *The Spanish Civil War, the Soviet Union and
   Communism* (New Haven, CT: Yale University Press, 2004),
   p. 295.
3 K. J. Holsti, *The State, War and the State of War* (Cambridge:
   Cambridge University Press, 1996), p. 3.
4 Steven R. David, 'Soviet Involvement in Third World Coups',
   International Security 11/1(1986): 4.
5 Chris Loveman, 'Assessing the Phenomenon of Proxy
   Intervention', *Conflict, Security and Development* 2/3(2002):
   31.
6 Mark A. Stoler, *Allies at War: Britain and America Against the Axis
   Powers, 1940–1945* (London: Hodder Arnold, 2005), p. 13.
7 Ibid., p. 15.
8 Ibid., p. 19. For an analysis of Lend-Lease, see David Reynolds,

The Creation of the Anglo-American Alliance, 1937–1941: A Study in Competitive Co-operation (London: Europa Publications, 1981), chapter 6.

9 Reynolds, *The Creation of the Anglo-American Alliance*, p. 288.

10 Stoler, *Allies at War*, p. 19.

11 Richard Ned Lebow, *Why Nations Fight* (Cambridge: Cambridge University Press, 2010), p. 18.

12 John Lewis Gaddis, *We Now Know: Rethinking Cold War History* (Oxford: Oxford University Press, 1997). In particular, see chapter 10.

13 S. Neil MacFarlane, *Superpower Rivalry and Third World Radicalism: The Idea of National Liberation* (London: Croom Helm, 1985), p. 3.

14 Celeste A. Wallander, 'Third World Conflict in Soviet Military Thought: Does the "New Thinking" Grow Prematurely Grey?', *World Politics* 42/1(1989): 34.

15 Richard E. Bissell, 'Soviet Use of Proxies in the Third World: The Case of Yemen', *Soviet Studies* 30/1(1978): 87–8.

16 Galia Golan, 'The Soviet Union and the PLO', *Adelphi Papers* 131(1977): 19–20.

17 Hans Morgenthau, 'To Intervene or Not to Intervene', *Foreign Affairs* 45/3(1967): 430.

18 Quoted in Lawrence Freedman, *Kennedy's Wars: Berlin, Cuba, Laos and Vietnam* (New York: Oxford University Press, 2002), p. 317.

19 Frank Costigliola, 'US Foreign Policy from Kennedy to Johnson', in Melvyn P. Leffler and Odd Arne Westad (eds), *The Cambridge History of the Cold War (Volume II: Crisis and Detente)* (Cambridge: Cambridge University Press, 2010), pp. 113–14.

20 Michael W. Doyle, 'Kant, Liberal Legacies and Foreign Affairs (Part 2)', *Philosophy and Public Affairs* 12/4(1983b): 330.

21 Ivo H. Daalder and James M. Lindsay, *American Unbound: The Rush Revolution in Foreign Policy* (Washington, DC: Brookings Institution Press, 2003), p. 2.

22 Stefan Halper and Jonathan Clarke, *America Alone: The Neo-Conservatives and the Global Order* (New York: Cambridge University Press, 2005), p. 4.

23 Quoted in Freedman, *Kennedy's Wars*, p. 318.

24 Ibid., p. 330.

25 Odd Arne Westad, *The Global Cold War: Third World Intervention*

and the Making of Our Times (Cambridge: Cambridge University Press, 2007), p. 4.
26 Philip Towle, 'The Strategy of War by Proxy', *RUSI Journal* 126/1(1981): 21.
27 John Mueller, *Retreat from Doomsday: The Obsolescence of Major War* (New York: Basic Books, 1989), p. 13.
28 Congressional Research Service (CRS) Report for Congress, 'Conventional Arms Transfers to Developing Nations, 1999–2006' (Washington, DC: 26 September 2007), p. 4.
29 Ibid., p. 6.
30 Congressional Research Service (CRS) Issue Brief for Congress, 'Israel: US Foreign Assistance' (Washington, DC: 7 March 2005), p. 1.
31 John J. Mearsheimer and Stephen M. Walt, 'The Israel Lobby and US Foreign Policy', *Middle East Policy* 13/3(2006): 31.
32 CRS, 'Israel: US Foreign Assistance', p. 6.
33 Ibid., p. 7.
34 Mearsheimer and Walt, 'The Israel Lobby and US Foreign Policy', p. 32.
35 Christopher Coker, *War in an Age of Risk* (Cambridge: Polity, 2009), p. viii.
36 Ibid., p. 7.
37 Charles S. Gochman and Russell J. Leng, 'Realpolitik and the Road to War: An Analysis of Attributes and Behaviour', *International Studies Quarterly* 27/1(1983): 100.
38 Alan J. Kuperman, 'The Stinger Missile and US Intervention in Afghanistan', *Political Science Quarterly* 114/2(1999): 225.
39 Bruce Porter, *The USSR in Third World Conflicts: Soviet Arms and Diplomacy in Local Wars, 1945–80* (Cambridge: Cambridge University Press, 1984), p. 227.
40 Robert Jervis, 'Cooperation Under the Security Dilemma', *World Politics* 30/2(1978): 169.
41 Ibid., pp. 174–5.

CHAPTER 3 WHO ENGAGES IN PROXY WAR?

1 William Rosenau, 'The Kennedy Administration, US Foreign Internal Assistance, and the Challenge of "Subterranean War", 1961–63', *Small Wars and Insurgencies* 14/3(2003): 65.

2 John Lewis Gaddis, 'Grand Strategies in the Cold War', in Melvyn
   P.Leffler and Odd Arne Westad (eds), *The Cambridge History of the
   Cold War (Volume II: Crisis and Detente)* (Cambridge: Cambridge
   University Press, 2010), p. 8.
3 Janice Gross Stein, 'Proxy Wars – How Superpowers End
   Them: The Diplomacy of War Termination in the Middle East',
   International Journal 35 (Summer 1980): 481.
4 Gaddis, 'Grand Strategies in the Cold War', p. 13.
5 Raymond L. Garthoff, *Detente and Confrontation: American–Soviet
   Relations from Nixon to Reagan*, revsd edn (Washington, DC: The
   Brookings Institution, 1994), p. 557.
6 Ibid., pp. 558–60.
7 Jiri Valenta, 'The Soviet-Cuban Intervention in Angola, 1975',
   Studies in Comparative Communism 11/1&2(1978): 10–11.
8 Garthoff, *Detente and Confrontation*, p. 567.
9 Ibid., p. 564.
10 Ibid., p. 576.
11 Ibid., p. 581.
12 Doran Zimmermann, 'Calibrating Disorder: Iran's Role in Iraq
   and the Coalition Response, 2003–2006', *Civil Wars* 9/1(2007):
   8.
13 Ibid., p. 15.
14 House of Commons Defence Select Committee, 'UK Operations
   in Iraq', Thirteenth Report of Session 2005–06, HC 1241 (August
   2006), p. 8, para.17.
15 Congressional Research Service (CRS), 'Report for Congress:
   Iran's Influence in Iraq' (Washington, DC: 12 September 2007),
   p. 3.
16 Ewan MacAskill, Ian Traynor and Robert Tait, 'US Accuses
   Highest Levels in Iran of Supplying Deadly Weapons to Iraqi
   Insurgents', *Guardian*, 12 February 2007, available at: <http://
   www.guardian.co.uk/world/2007/feb/12/topstories3.iran>.
17 Simon Tisdall, 'Iran's Secret Plan for Summer Offensive to Force
   US out of Iraq', *Guardian*, 22 May 2007, available at: <http://
   www.guardian.co.uk/world/2007/may/22/iraq.topstories3>.
18 CRS, 'Iran's Influence in Iraq', p. 4.
19 Ibid., p. 2.
20 Michael Knight and Ed Williams, 'The Calm Before the Storm: The
   British Experience in Southern Iraq' (The Washington Institute for
   Near East Policy, Policy Focus 66, February 2007), p. 28.

21 Transcript from evidence of Tony Blair at Chilcot Iraq Inquiry, 29 January 2010, at <http://www.iraqinquiry.org.uk/media/43909/100129-blair.pdf>, p. 182, lines 15–18.
22 As enunciated by Geraint Hughes, *My Enemy's Enemy: Proxy Warfare in International Politics* (Brighton: Sussex Academic Press, 2012), p. 10.
23 Emile El-Hokayem, 'Hizballah and Syria: Outgrowing the Proxy Relationship', *The Washington Quarterly* 30/2(2007): 35.
24 Graham E. Fuller, 'The Hizballah-Iran Connection: Model for Sunni Resistance', *The Washington Quarterly* 30/1 (Winter 2006–07): 139.
25 Ibid., p. 142.
26 Zimmermann, 'Calibrating Disorder', p. 14.
27 Marie Colvin, 'Hamas Wages Iran's Proxy War on Israel', *The Sunday Times*, 9 March 2008, available at: <http://www.thesundaytimes.co.uk/sto/news/world_news/article82296.ece>.
28 Ibid.
29 Ryan Clarke, 'Lashkar-i-Taiba: Roots, Logistics, Partnerships and the Fallacy of Subservient Proxies', *Terrorism and Political Violence* 22/3(2010): 394.
30 Ariel I. Ahram, *Proxy Warriors: The Rise and Fall of State-Sponsored Militias* (Stanford, CA: Stanford University Press, 2011), p. 2.
31 Gerard Prunier, 'Rebel Movements and Proxy Warfare: Uganda, Sudan and the Congo (1986–1999)', *African Affairs* 103/412(2004): 359.
32 Roger Dean, 'Rethinking the Civil War in Sudan', *Civil Wars* 3/1(2000): 82.
33 Prunier, 'Rebel Movements and Proxy Warfare', p. 366.
34 Ibid, pp. 373–7.
35 Ibid, p. 381.

CHAPTER 4 HOW ARE PROXY WARS FOUGHT?

1 For a summary of these debates and hypotheses, see Jeffrey A. Friedman, 'Manpower and Counterinsurgency: Empirical Foundations for Theory and Doctrine', *Security Studies* 20/4(2011): 556–91.
2 Bruce D. Porter, *The USSR in Third World Conflicts: Soviet Arms*

and Diplomacy in Local Wars, 1945–1980 (Cambridge: Cambridge University Press, 1984), p. 229.

3 Ibid., p. 230.

4 Christopher Stevens, 'The Soviet Union and Angola', *African Affairs* 75/299(1976): 144.

5 Steven R. David, 'Soviet Involvement in Third World Coups', *International Security* 11/1(1986): 8.

6 Stevens, 'The Soviet Union and Angola', p. 145.

7 David, 'Soviet Involvement in Third World Coups', p. 9.

8 Ibid., p. 7.

9 Ibid., p. 12.

10 *Documents on British Policy Overseas*, Series 1, Volume VIII, 'Britain and China, 1945–50', Chapter IV (1948), Document no. 35 ('Minute from Sir O. Sargent to Mr Attlee', 1 January 1948) and Document no.50 ('UK Delegation to UN General Assembly [Paris] to Mr Bevin', 19 November 1948).

11 Porter, *The USSR in Third World Conflicts*, p. 21.

12 Ibid., p. 30.

13 William Rosenau, 'The Kennedy Administration, US Foreign Internal Assistance and the Challenge of "Subterranean War"', *Small Wars and Insurgencies* 14/3(2003): 82–5.

14 David, 'Soviet Involvement in Third World Coups', p. 7.

15 John Mackinlay, *The Insurgent Archipelago* (London: Hurst, 2009), p. 58.

16 Andrew Mumford, 'Intelligence Wars: Ireland and Afghanistan – The American Experience', *Civil Wars* 7/4(2005): 381–2 and 384–6.

17 Rosenau, 'The Kennedy Administration, US Foreign Internal Assistance and the Challenge of "Subterranean War"', p. 82.

18 Joseph Nye, *Soft Power: The Means to Success in World Politics* (New York: Public Affairs, 2004), p. x.

19 David, 'Soviet Involvement in Third World Coups', p. 7.

20 Nye, *Soft Power*, p. 2.

21 Ibid., p. 7.

22 For the full text of the Iraq Liberation Act (1998) go to: <http://www.gpo.gov/fdsys/pkg/BILLS-105hr4655enr/pdf/BILLS-105hr4655enr.pdf>.

23 Michael Gordon and Bernard Trainor, *Cobra II: The Insider Story of the Invasion and Occupation of Iraq* (London: Atlantic Books, 2006), pp. 12–13.

24 Gregory F. Treverton, *Covert Action: The Limits of Intervention in the Postwar World* (New York: Basic Books, 1987), p. 15.

25 Quoted in Thomas Ricks, *The Gamble: General David Petraeus and the American Military Adventure in Iraq, 2006–2008* (New York: Penguin, 2009), p. 205.

26 Ibid., pp. 202–3.

27 Major Niel Smith and Colonel Sean MacFarland, 'Anbar Awakens: The Tipping Point', *Military Review* 88 (March–April 2008): 44.

28 Ricks, *The Gamble*, p. 204.

29 Austin Long, 'The Anbar Awakening', *Survival* 50/2(2008): 67.

30 Ricks, *The Gamble*, p. 206.

31 Long, 'The Anbar Awakening', p. 68.

32 Charles G. Cogan, 'Partners in Time: The CIA and Afghanistan since 1979', *World Policy Journal* 10/2(1993): 74.

33 Steve Coll, *Ghost Wars: The Secret History of the CIA, Afghanistan and Bin Laden from the Soviet Invasion to September 10, 2001* (New York: Penguin, 2004), p. 46.

34 Quoted in Ibid, p. 51.

35 Raymond L. Garthoff, *Detente and Confrontation: American–Soviet Relations from Nixon to Reagan (Revised ed)* (Washington, DC: The Brookings Institute, 1994), p. 1073.

36 Coll, *Ghost Wars*, p. 66.

37 Dilip Hiro, *Between Marx and Muhammed: The Changing Face of Central Asia* (London: HarperCollins, 1995), p. 246.

38 Quoted in Alan J. Kuperman, 'The Stinger Missile and US Intervention in Afghanistan', *Political Science Quarterly* 114/2(1999): 227.

39 Ibid., p. 228.

40 Ibid., p. 246.

41 Ibid., p. 220.

42 John K. Cooley, *Unholy Wars: Afghanistan, America and International Terrorism (new edn)* (London: Pluto Press 2000), p. 4 (note 29).

43 Steve Galster, 'Afghanistan: Lessons from the Last War', Introductory Essay to the National Security Archive 'September 11th Sourcebook' (9 October 2001), at: <www2.gwu.edu/~nsarchiv/NSAEBB/NSAEBB57/essay2.html> (note 15).

44 Quoted in Coll, *Ghost Wars*, p. 99.

CHAPTER 5 THE FUTURE OF PROXY WAR

1 Philip Bobbitt, *The Shield of Achilles: War, Peace and the Course of History* (New York: Anchor Books, 2003), p. 331.
2 Ministry of Defence, *Future Character of Conflict* (Development Concepts and Doctrine Centre, February 2010), at: <www.mod.uk/DefenceInternet/MicroSite/DCDC/OurPublications/Concepts/FutureCharacterOfConflict.htm>.
3 Ivan Eland, 'Turn the War on Terrorism into a War by Proxy', CATO Institute (23 January 2002), at: <http://www.cato.org/pub_display.php?pub_id=6660>.
4 For a critical discussion of 'blowback' in the case of American foreign policy, see Chalmers Johnson, *Blowback: The Costs and Consequences of American Empire* (London: Time Warner, 2002).
5 Colin Gray, 'The Twenty-First Century Security Environment and the Future of War', *Parameters* 38 (Winter 2008–09): 17.
6 Department of Defense (DoD), *Sustaining US Global Leadership: Priorities for 21st Century Defense* (January 2012), p. i , at: <http://www.defense.gov/news/Defense_Strategic_Guidance.pdf>.
7 BBC News online, 'Obama Unveils New Strategy for "Leaner" US Military', 5 January 2012, at: <http://www.bbc.co.uk/news/world-us-canada-16430405?print=true>.
8 DoD, *Sustaining US Global Leadership*, pp. 3–5.
9 Christopher Coker, *War in an Age of Risk* (Cambridge: Polity, 2009), p. 27.
10 Jose L. Gomez del Prado, 'Private Military and Security Companies and the UN Working Group on the Use of Mercenaries', *Journal of Conflict and Security Law* 13/3(2009): 438.
11 Anna Leander, 'The Power to Construct International Security: On the Significance of Private Military Companies', *Millennium* 33/3(2005): 806.
12 P. W. Singer, 'Corporate Warriors: The Rise of the Privatized Military Industry and its Ramifications for International Security, *International Security* 26/3(2001–02): 193.
13 David Shearer, 'Private Armies and Military Intervention', *Adelphi Paper* 316(1998): 10.
14 Clive Walker and Dave Whyte, 'Contracting Out War? Private Military Companies, Law and Regulation in the United Kingdom', *International and Comparative Law Quarterly* 54/2(2005): 659.

15 Quoted in Singer, 'Corporate Warriors', p. 195.
16 Ibid., p. 217.
17 Adam Ciralsky, 'Tycoon, Contractor, Soldier, Spy', *Vanity Fair* (January 2010), pp. 100–4.
18 Christopher Kinsey, *Corporate Soldiers and International Security* (Abindgon: Routledge, 2006), pp. 15–16.
19 Shawn Engbrecht, *America's Covert Warriors: Inside the World of Private Military Contractors* (Dulles, VA: Potomac Books, 2011), p. 4.
20 Del Prado, 'Private Military and Security Companies', p. 437.
21 US Congressional Budget Office (CBO) Report, 'Contractors' Support of US Operations in Iraq', (Washington, DC: August 2008), pp. 1–2.
22 Engbrecht, *America's Covert Warriors*, p. 4.
23 US CBO report, 'Contractors' Support of US Operations in Iraq', p. 2.
24 Del Prado, 'Private Military and Security Companies', p. 436.
25 Which remains unenforceable given that none of the five permanent members of the UN Security Council has yet to sign it.
26 Del Prado, 'Private Military and Security Companies', p. 436.
27 Engbrecht, *America's Covert Warriors*, p. 95.
28 Ibid., p. 13.
29 Singer, 'Corporate Warriors', p. 187.
30 Engbrecht, *America's Covert Warriors*, p. xvi.
31 Singer, 'Corporate Warriors', p. 212.
32 Ibid., p. 213.
33 Jim Giles, 'Are States Unleashing the Dogs of Cyber War?', *New Scientist* 2791 (December 2010), available at: <http://www.newscientist.com/article/mg20827915.100-are-states-unleashing-the-dogs-of-cyber-war.html>.
34 Center for Strategic and International Studies report, 'Significant Cyber Incidents Since 2006', at: <http://csis.org/files/publication/110621_Significant_Cyber_Incidents_Since_ 2006.pdf>.
35 Nick Hopkins, 'China "Targets Nato Chief" in Facebook Spying Operation', *The Observer*, 11 March 2012, available at: <http://www.guardian.co.uk/world/2012/mar/11/china-spies-facebook-attack-nato>.
36 BBC News online, 'MI5 Fighting "Astonishing" Level of

Cyber-attacks', 25 June 2012, at: <http://www.bbc.co.uk/news/uk-18586681?print=true>.

37 For a thorough expose of the Stuxnet plan, see David Sanger, 'Obama Order Sped Up Wave of Cyberattacks Against Iran', *The New York Times*, 1 June 2012, available at: <http://www.nytimes.com/2012/06/01/world/middleeast/obama-ordered-wave-of-cyberattacks-against-iran.html?pagewanted=all>.

38 Ibid.

39 James P. Farwell and Rafal Rohozinski, 'Stuxnet and the Future of Cyber War', *Survival* 53/1(2011): 28 and 35.

40 Associated Press, 'China Victim of 500,000 Cyber Attacks in 2010, Says Security Agency', *Guardian*, 9 August 2011, available at: <http://www.guardian.co.uk/world/2011/aug/09/china-cyber-attacks>.

41 For a sample of such debate, see G. John Ikenberry, 'The Future of the Liberal World Order', *Foreign Affairs* 90/3(2011): 56–68; Charles Glaser, 'Will China's Rise Lead to War?', *Foreign Affairs* 90/2(2011): 80–91; Wang Wisi, 'China's Search for a Grand Strategy', *Foreign Affairs* 90/2(2011): 68–79; Thomas J. Christensen, 'The Advantages of an Assertive China', *Foreign Affairs* 90/2(2011): 54–67; Dean Cheng, 'Chinese Views on Deterrence', *Joint Forces Quarterly* 60/1(2011): 92–4; James Kurth, 'Confronting a Powerful China with Western Characteristics', *Orbis* 56/1(2012): 39–59; James Dobbins, 'War with China', *Survival* 54/4(2012): 7–24; and Lanxin Xiang, 'China and the "Pivot"', *Survival* 54/5(2012): 113–28.

42 Michael W. Doyle, 'Kant, Liberal Legacies and Foreign Affairs (Part 1)', *Philosophy and Public Affairs* 12/3(1983a): 233–4.

43 DoD, *Sustaining US Global Leadership*, p. 2.

44 Keith B. Richburg, 'China Military Spending to Top $100 Billion in 2012, Alarming Neighbours', *The Washington Post*, 4 March 2012, available at: <http://www.washingtonpost.com/world/china-military-spending-to-top-100-billion-this-year/2012/03/04/gIQAJRnypR_story.html>.

45 JoAnne Wagner, '"Going Out": Is China's Skilful Use of Soft Power in Sub-Saharan Africa a Threat to US Interests?', *Joint Forces Quarterly* 64/1(2012): 99.

46 Ibid., p. 100.

47 David Shambaugh, 'Coping with a Conflicted China', *The Washington Quarterly* 34/1(2011): 24.

48 S. Neil MacFarlane, *Superpower Rivalry and Third World Radicalism: The Idea of National Liberation* (London: Croom Helm, 1985), p. 137.
49 For further advocacy of such a position, see Mark O. Yeisley, 'Bipolarity, Proxy Wars and the Rise of China', *Strategic Studies Quarterly* 5/4(2011): 75–91.
50 Chris Alden, 'China in Africa', *Survival* 47/3(2005): 148.
51 Wagner, 'Going Out', p. 101.
52 Ibid., p. 102.
53 Quoted in Ibid., p. 102.
54 Qiao Liang and Wang Xiansui, 'Unrestricted Warfare' (Beijing: People's Liberation Army Literature and Arts Publishing House, February 1999), pp. 6 and 12, available at <http://militarydispatch.com/publications/unrestrictedwarfare.pdf >.

CONCLUSION: THE CONTINUING APPEAL OF PROXY WAR

1   Kalevi J. Holsti, *The State, War and the State of War* (Cambridge: Cambridge University Press, 1996), p. 127.
2   Quoted in BBC News online, 'Syria Unrest: Opposition Seeks Arms Pledge', 24 February 2012, at: <http://www.bbc.co.uk/news/world-middle-east-17144805?print=true>.
3   Quoted in BBC News online, 'Iraq's Maliki Warns of Syria "Proxy War"', 29 March 2012, at <http://www.bbc.co.uk/news/world-middle-east-17544431?print=true>.
4   BBC News online, 'UK Doubles Aid to Syrian Opposition Groups', 30 March 2012, at <http://www.bbc.co.uk/news/uk-17558417?print=true>.
5   For a full webcast of Panetta's testimony see <http://senate.gov/fplayers/jw57/urlMP4Player.cfm?fn=armed037&st=1120&dur=9960>.
6   BBC News online, 'Syria Conflict: UK to Give an Extra £5m to Opposition Groups', 10 August 2012, at <http://www.bbc.co.uk/news/uk-19205204?print=true>.
7   BBC News online, 'Ship "Carrying Russian Attack Helicopters to Syria" Halted off Scotland', 19 June 2012, at <http://www.bbc.co.uk/news/uk-scotland-highlands-islands-18503421?print=true>.
8   BBC News online, 'Syrian Plane Had Illegal Cargo, Says Turkey's

Davutoglu', 11 October 2012, at <http://www.bbc.co.uk/news/
world-europe-19906578?print=true>.

9 *Foreign Relations of the United States, 1955–57*: Foreign Aid
and Economic Defense Policy (Vol. X), Document No.9,
'Memorandum of Discussion at the 267th Meeting of the
National Security Council, Camp David, Maryland, 21 November
1955,' p. 34.

10 Bruce D. Porter, *The USSR in Third World Conflicts: Soviet Arms
and Diplomacy in Local Wars, 1945–80* (Cambridge: Cambridge
University Press, 1984), pp. 236–7.

11 Celeste A. Wallander, 'Third World Conflict in Soviet Military
Thought: Does the "New Thinking" Grow Prematurely Grey?',
World Politics 42/1(1989): 33.

12 For discussion of 'hybrid wars', see Frank Hoffman, 'Conflict
in the Twenty-First Century: The Rise of Hybrid Wars'
(Potomac Institute for Policy Studies, 2007), at <http://www.
potomacinstitute.org/images/stories/publications/potomac_
hybridwar_0108.pdf>. For a discussion of the intra-military
friction in relation to the centrality of counter-insurgency doctrine
to future US war-fighting, see Elisabeth Bumiller, 'West Point
is Divided on a War Doctrine's Fate', *New York Times*, 27 May
2012, available at: <http://www.nytimes.com/2012/05/28/
world/at-west-point-asking-if-a-war-doctrine-was-worth-it.
html?pagewanted=all>.

13 Jon Abdink, 'Ethiopia–Eritrea: Proxy Wars and the Prospects
of Peace in the Horn of Africa', *Journal of Contemporary African
Studies* 21/3(2003): 407.

14 'Minister: Suicide Bomber a Handicapped Child', at <www.
msnbc.com>, 31 January 2005.

15 Henry McDonald, 'Car Bomb Explodes at Ulster Army Barracks',
Guardian, 12 April 2010, available at: <http://www.guardian.co.uk/
uk/2010/apr/12/northern-ireland-justice-minister-david-ford>.

16 A transcript of the declaration, announced as a means of
establishing the 'World Front for Jihad Against the Jews and
Crusaders', can be found in Fred Halliday, *Two Hours That Shook
the World – September 11, 2001: Causes and Consequences* (London:
Saqi Books, 2002), Appendix 1, pp. 217–19.

17 S. Neil MacFarlane, *Superpower Rivalry and Third World
Radicalism: The Idea of National Liberation* (London: Croom
Helm, 1985), p. 5.

18 Stephen R. Weissman, 'CIA Covert Action in Zaire and Angola: Patterns and Consequences', *Political Science Quarterly* 94/2(1979): 264.
19 Andrew S. Natsios, 'To Give South Sudan a Chance at Peace, Supply it with Weapons', *The Washington Post*, 13 May 2012, available at: <http://www.washingtonpost.com/opinions/to-stop-the-war-on-south-sudan-the-us-should-send-weapons/2012/05/11/gIQAywIkIU_story.html>.
20 Amnesty International Report, *South Sudan: Overshadowed Conflict* (London: June 2012), p. 8.
21 Stanley G. Payne, *The Spanish Civil War, the Soviet Union and Communism* (New Haven, CT: Yale University Press, 2004), p. 295.
22 Hugh Thomas, *The Spanish Civil War*, 4th edn (London: Penguin, 2003), p. 915.
23 Chalmers Johnson, *Blowback: The Costs and Consequences of American Empire* (London: Time Warner, 2002), pp. 17–18.
24 Ibid., pp. 237–8.
25 Alan J. Kuperman, 'The Stinger Missile and US Intervention in Afghanistan', *Political Science Quarterly* 114/2(1999): 253.
26 Ibid, p. 254.
27 Robert D. Kaplan, *Soldiers of God: With Islamic Warriors in Afghanistan and Pakistan*, new edn (New York: Vintage Books 2001), p. 11.
28 *9/11 Commission Report*, authorized edn (New York: W.W Norton 2004), p. 103.
29 Quoted in John K. Cooley, *Unholy Wars: Afghanistan, America and International Terrorism*, new edn (London: Pluto Press 2000), p. 20 (note 29).
30 Andrew Mumford, 'Intelligence Wars: Ireland and Afghanistan – The American Experience', *Civil Wars* 7/4(2005): 390.
31 Kaplan, *Soldiers of God*, p. xvii (note 45).

Bibliography

PRIMARY SOURCES

9/11 Commission Report (authorized edn) 2004 (New York: W.W Norton).

Congressional Research Service (CRS), 2005 'Issue Brief for Congress: Israel – US Foreign Assistance' (Washington, DC: 7 March), available at: <http://www.fas.org/sgp/crs/mideast/IB85066.pdf>.

Congressional Research Service (CRS), 2007 'Report for Congress: Iran's Influence in Iraq' (Washington, DC: 12 September), available at: <http://fpc.state.gov/documents/organization/91004.pdf>.

Congressional Research Service (CRS), 2007 'Report for Congress: Conventional Arms Transfers to Developing Nations, 1999–2006' (Washington, DC: 26 September), available at: <http://www.fas.org/sgp/crs/weapons/RL34187.pdf>.

Department of Defense (DoD), 2012 *Sustaining US Global Leadership: Priorities for 21st Century Defense* (January) (Washington, DC: The Pentagon).

Documents on British Policy Overseas, 2002 Series 1, Volume VIII, 'Britain and China, 1945–50' (London: Her Majesty's Stationery Office).

Foreign Relations of the United States, 1989 Vol. X, '1955–57: Foreign Aid and Economic Defense Policy' (Washington, DC: US State Department).

House of Commons Defence Select Committee, 2006 'UK Operations in Iraq', Thirteenth Report of Session 2005–06, HC 1241 (August).

Ministry of Defence (MoD), 2010 *Future Character of Conflict* (Development Concepts and Doctrine Centre, February).

US Congressional Budget Office Report, 2008 'Contractors' Support of US Operations in Iraq' (Washington, DC: August), available at: <http://www.cbo.gov/sites/default/files/cbofiles/ftpdocs/96xx/doc 9688/08-12-iraqcontractors.pdf>.

SECONDARY SOURCES

Books

Ahram, Ariel I., 2011 *Proxy Warriors: The Rise and Fall of State-Sponsored Militias* (Stanford, CA: Stanford University Press).

Beevor, Antony, 2006 *The Battle for Spain: The Spanish Civil War, 1936–1939* (New York: Penguin).

Bellamy, Alex, 2009 *Responsibility to Protect* (Cambridge: Polity).

Blainey, Geoffrey, 1973 *The Causes of War* (London: Macmillan).

Bobbitt, Philip, 2003 *The Shield of Achilles: War, Peace and the Course of History* (New York: Anchor Books).

Bull, Hedley, 1984 *Intervention in World Politics* (Oxford: Oxford University Press).

Coker, Christopher, 2009 *War in an Age of Risk* (Cambridge: Polity).

Coll, Steve, 2004 *Ghost Wars: The Secret History of the CIA, Afghanistan and Bin Laden from the Soviet Invasion to September 10, 2001* (New York: Penguin).

Cooley, John K., 2000 *Unholy Wars: Afghanistan, America and International Terrorism (new ed)* (London: Pluto Press).

Daalder, Ivo H. and James M. Lindsay, 2003 *American Unbound: The Rush Revolution in Foreign Policy* (Washington, DC: Brookings Institution Press).

Eckstein, Harry (ed.), 1964 *Internal War: Problems and Approaches* (New York: Free Press of Glencoe).

Engbrecht, Shawn, 2011 *America's Covert Warriors: Inside the World of Private Military Contractors* (Dulles, VA: Potomac Books).

Foreman, Amanda, 2011 *A World on Fire: An Epic History of Two Nations Divided* (London: Penguin).

Freedman, Lawrence, 2002 *Kennedy's Wars: Berlin, Cuba, Laos and Vietnam* (New York: Oxford University Press).

Gaddis, John Lewis, 1997 *We Now Know: Rethinking Cold War History* (Oxford: Oxford University Press).

Garthoff, Raymond L., 1994 *Detente and Confrontation: American-Soviet Relations from Nixon to Reagan (revised edition)* (Washington, DC: The Brookings Institution).

Gordon, Michael, and Bernard Trainor, 2006 *Cobra II: The Insider Story of the Invasion and Occupation of Iraq* (London: Atlantic Books).

Halliday, Fred, 2002 *Two Hours That Shook the World – September 11, 2001: Causes and Consequences* (London: Saqi Books).

Halper, Stefan, and Jonathan Clarke, 2005 *America Alone: The Neo-Conservatives and the Global Order* (New York: Cambridge University Press).

Halperin, Morton, 1963 *Limited War in the Nuclear Age* (New York: John Wiley & Sons).

Hiro, Dilip, 1995 *Between Marx and Muhammed: The Changing Face of Central Asia* (London: HarperCollins).

Holsti, Kalevi J., 1996 *The State, War and the State of War* (Cambridge: Cambridge University Press).

Howson, Gerald, 1998 *Arms for Spain: The Untold Story of the Spanish Civil War* (London: John Murray).

Hughes, Geraint, 2012 *My Enemy's Enemy: Proxy Warfare in International Politics* (Brighton: Sussex Academic Press).

Innes, Michael (ed.), 2012 *Making Sense of Proxy Wars: States, Surrogates and the Use of Force* (Dulles, VA: Potomac Books).

Johnson, Chalmers, 2002 *Blowback: The Costs and Consequences of American Empire* (London: Time Warner).

Kanet, Roger E. (ed.), 1974 *The Soviet Union and the Developing Nations* (Baltimore: Johns Hopkins University Press).

Kaplan, Robert D., 2001 *Soldiers of God: With Islamic Warriors in Afghanistan and Pakistan (new ed)* (New York: Vintage Books).

Karnow, Stanley, 1997 *Vietnam: A History* (London: Penguin).

Kinsey, Christopher, 2006 *Corporate Soldiers and International Security* (Abindgon: Routledge).

Lebow, Richard Ned, 2010 *Why Nations Fight* (Cambridge: Cambridge University Press).

Leffler, Mervyn P. and Odd Arne Westad (ed.), 2010 *The Cambridge History of the Cold War (Volume II: Crisis and Detente)* (Cambridge: Cambridge University Press).

MacFarlane, S. Neil, 1985 *Superpower Rivalry and Third World Radicalism: The Idea of National Liberation* (London: Croom Helm).

Mackinlay, John, 2009 *The Insurgent Archipelago* (London: Hurst).

Mueller, John, 1989 *Retreat from Doomsday: The Obsolescence of Major War* (New York: Basic Books).

Nye, Joesph, 2004 *Soft Power: The Means to Success in World Politics* (New York: Public Affairs).

Payne, Stanley G., 2004 *The Spanish Civil War, the Soviet Union and Communism* (New Haven, CT: Yale University Press).

Porter, Bruce D., 1984 *The USSR in Third World Conflicts: Soviet Arms* and Diplomacy in Local Wars, 1945–80 (Cambridge: Cambridge University Press).

Regan, Patrick M., 2002 Civil Wars and Foreign Powers: Outside Intervention in Intrastate Conflict (Ann Arbor, MI: University of Michigan Press).

Reynolds, David, 1981 The Creation of the Anglo-American Alliance, 1937–1941: A Study in Competitive Co-operation (London: Europa Publications).

Ricks, Thomas, 2009 The Gamble: General David Petraeus and the American Military Adventure in Iraq, 2006–2008 (New York: Penguin).

Singer, P. W., 2010 Wired for War: The Robotics Revolution and Conflict in the Twenty-First Century (New York: Penguin).

Stiglitz, Joseph, and Linda Bilmes, 2009 The Three Trillion Dollar War: The True Cost of the Iraq Conflict (London: Penguin).

Stoler, Marc A., 2005 Allies at War: Britain and America Against the Axis Powers, 1940–1945 (London: Hodder Arnold).

Thomas, Hugh, 2003 The Spanish Civil War (4th edition) (London: Penguin).

Treverton, Gregory F., 1987 Covert Action: The Limits of Intervention in the Postwar World (New York: Basic Books).

Vasquez, John, 2009 The War Puzzle Revisited (Cambridge: Cambridge University Press).

Westad, Odd Arne, 2007 The Global Cold War: Third World Interventions and the Making of Our Times (Cambridge: Cambridge University Press).

Wheeler, Nicholas, 2000 Saving Strangers: Humanitarian Intervention in International Society (Oxford: Oxford University Press).

Articles

Abdink, Jon, 2003 'Ethiopia–Eritrea: Proxy Wars and the Prospects of Peace in the Horn of Africa', Journal of Contemporary African Studies 21/3: 407–25.

Alden, Chris, 2005 'China in Africa', Survival 47/3: 147–64.

Bar-Siman-Tov, Yaacov, 1984 'The Strategy of War by Proxy', Cooperation and Conflict 19: 263–73.

Bissell, Richard E., 1978 'Soviet Use of Proxies in the Third World: The Case of Yemen', Soviet Studies 30/1: 87–106.

Cheng, Dean, 2011 'Chinese Views on Deterrence', Joint Forces Quarterly 60/1: 92–4.

Christensen, Thomas J., 2011 'The Advantages of an Assertive China', *Foreign Affairs* 90/2: 54–67.

Clarke, Ryan, 2010 'Lashkar-i-Taiba: Roots, Logistics, Partnerships and the Fallacy of Subservient Proxies', *Terrorism and Political Violence* 22/3: 394–417.

Cogan, Charles G., 1993 'Partners in Time: The CIA and Afghanistan since 1979', *World Policy Journal* 10/2: 73–82.

David, Steven R., 1986 'Soviet Involvement in Third World Coups', *International Security* 11/1: 3–26.

Davis, Nathaniel, 1978 'The Angola Decision of 1975: A Personal Memoir', *Foreign Affairs* 57/1: 109–24.

Dean, Roger, 2000 'Rethinking the Civil War in Sudan', *Civil Wars* 3/1: 71–91.

Dobbins, James, 2012 'War with China', *Survival* 54/4: 7–24.

Doyle, Michael W., 1983a 'Kant, Liberal Legacies and Foreign Affairs (Part 1)', *Philosophy and Public Affairs* 12/3: 205–35.

Doyle, Michael W., 1983b 'Kant, Liberal Legacies and Foreign Affairs (Part 2)', *Philosophy and Public Affairs* 12/4: 323–53.

Dunér, Bertil, 1981 'Proxy Intervention in Civil Wars', *Journal of Peace Research* 18/4: 353–61.

Economides, Spyros, 2000 'The Greek and Spanish Civil Wars: A Comparison', *Civil Wars* 3/2: 89–105.

El-Hokayem, Emile, 2007 'Hizballah and Syria: Outgrowing the Proxy Relationship', *The Washington Quarterly* 30/2: 35–52.

Farwell, James P., and Rafal Rohozinski, 2011 'Stuxnet and the Future of Cyber War', *Survival* 53/1: 23–40.

Friedman, Jeffrey A., 2011 'Manpower and Counterinsurgency: Empirical Foundations for Theory and Doctrine', *Security Studies* 20/4: 556–91.

Fuller, Graham E., 2006–07 'The Hizballah-Iran Connection: Model for Sunni Resistance', *The Washington Quarterly* 30/1(Winter): 139–50.

Galan Carpenter, Ted, and Malou Innocent, 2007–08 'The Iraq War and Iranian Power', *Survival* 49/4: 67–82.

Glaser, Charles, 2011 'Will China's Rise Lead to War?', *Foreign Affairs* 90/2: 80–91.

Gochman, Charles S. and Russell J. Leng, 1983 'Realpolitik and the Road to War: An Analysis of Attributes and Behaviour', *International Studies Quarterly* 27/1: 97–120.

Golan, Galia, 1977 'The Soviet Union and the PLO', *Adelphi Papers* 131.

Gomez del Prado, Jose L., 2009 'Private Military and Security Companies and the UN Working Group on the Use of Mercenaries', *Journal of Conflict and Security Law* 13/3: 429–50.

Gray, Colin, 2008–09 'The Twenty-First Century Security Environment and the Future of War', *Parameters* 38 (Winter): 14–26.

Gross Stein, Janice, 1980 'Proxy Wars – How Superpowers End Them: The Diplomacy of War Termination in the Middle East', *International Journal* 35 (Summer): 478–519.

Ikenberry, G. John, 2011 'The Future of the Liberal World Order', *Foreign Affairs* 90/3: 56–68.

Interview with Leon Panetta, 2009 'Obama's Middle East Strategy', *New Perspectives Quarterly* 26/3: 33–9.

Jervis, Robert, 1978 'Cooperation Under the Security Dilemma', *World Politics* 30/2: 167–214.

Knight, Michael, and Ed Williams, 2007 'The Calm Before the Storm: The British Experience in Southern Iraq' (The Washington Institute for Near East Policy, *Policy Focus* 66, February).

Kuperman, Alan J., 1999 'The Stinger Missile and US Intervention in Afghanistan', *Political Science Quarterly* 114/2: 219–63.

Kurth, James, 2012 'Confronting a Powerful China with Western Characteristics', *Orbis* 56/1: 39–59.

Leander, Anna, 2005 'The Power to Construct International Security: On the Significance of Private Military Companies', *Millennium* 33/3: 803–26.

Long, Austin, 2008 'The Anbar Awakening', *Survival* 50/2: 67–94.

Loveman, Chris, 2002 'Assessing the Phenomenon of Proxy Intervention', *Conflict, Security and Development* 2/3: 29–48.

Mearsheimer, John J, and Stephen M. Walt, 2006 'The Israel Lobby and US Foreign Policy', *Middle East Policy* 13/3: 29–87.

Morgenthau, Hans, 1967 'To Intervene or Not to Intervene', *Foreign Affairs* 45/3: 425–36.

Mumford, Andrew, 2005 'Intelligence Wars: Ireland and Afghanistan – The American Experience', *Civil Wars* 7/4: 377–95.

Mumford, Andrew, 2011 'Counter-Insurgency Research: A Case of Recurring Amnesia', *International Studies Today* 1/1: 1–2.

Pearson, Frederic S., 1974 'Foreign Military Interventions and Domestic Disputes', *International Studies Quarterly* 18/3: 259–90.

Prunier, Gerard, 2004 'Rebel Movements and Proxy Warfare: Uganda, Sudan and the Congo (1986–1999)', *African Affairs* 103/412: 359–83.

Regan, Patrick M., 2002 'Third Party Intervention and the Duration of Intrastate Conflict', *Journal of Conflict Resolution* 46/1: 55–73.

Rosenau, William, 2003 'The Kennedy Administration, US Foreign Internal Assistance, and the Challenge of 'Subterranean War', 1961–63', *Small Wars and Insurgencies* 14/3: 65–99.

Rudgers, David F., 2003 'The Origins of Covert Action', *Journal of Contemporary History* 35/2: 249–62.

Schaub, Gary and Volker Franke, 2009–10 'Contractors as Military Professionals?', *Parameters* (Winter): 88–104.

Shambaugh, David, 2011 'Coping with a Conflicted China', *The Washington Quarterly* 34/1: 7–27.

Shearer, David, 1998 'Private Armies and Military Intervention', *Adelphi Paper*, 316.

Singer, P. W., 2001–02 'Corporate Warriors: The Rise of the Privatized Military Industry and its Ramifications for International Security, *International Security* 26/3: 186–220.

Smith, Alastair, 1996 'To Intervene or Not to Intervene: A Biased Decision', *Journal of Conflict Resolution* 40/1: 16–40.

Smith, Maj. Niel and Col. Sean MacFarland, 2008 'Anbar Awakens: The Tipping Point', *Military Review* (March–April): 41–52.

Solarz, Stephen J., 1986 'When to Intervene', *Foreign Policy* 63: 20–39.

Stevens, Christopher, 1976 'The Soviet Union and Angola', *African Affairs* 75/299: 137–51.

Tillema, Harold, 1989 'Foreign Overt Military Intervention in the Nuclear Age', *Journal of Peace Research* 26/2: 179–96.

Towle, Philip, 1981 'The Strategy of War by Proxy', *RUSI Journal* 126/1: 21–6.

Valenta, Jiri, 1978 'The Soviet-Cuban Intervention in Angola, 1975', *Studies in Comparative Communism* 11/1&2: 3–33.

Wagner, JoAnne, 2012 '"Going Out": Is China's Skilful Use of Soft Power in Sub-Saharan Africa a Threat to US Interests?', *Joint Forces Quarterly* 64/1: 99–106.

Walker, Clive and Dave Whyte, 2005 'Contracting Out War? Private Military Companies, Law and Regulation in the United Kingdom', *International and Comparative Law Quarterly* 54/2: 651–90.

Wallander, Celleste, A., 1989 'Third World Conflict in Soviet Military Thought: Does the "New Thinking" Grow Prematurely Grey?', *World Politics* 42/1: 31–63.

Weissman, Stephen R., 1979 'CIA Covert Action in Zaire and Angola:

Patterns and Consequences', *Political Science Quarterly* 94/2: 263–86.

Williams, Brian Glyn, 2010 'The CIA's Covert Predator Drone Strikes in Pakistan, 2004–2010: The History of an Assassination Campaign', *Studies in Conflict and Terrorism* 33/10: 871–92.

Wisi, Wang, 2011 'China's Search for a Grand Strategy', *Foreign Affairs* 90/2: 68–79.

Xiang, Lanxin, 2012 'China and the "Pivot"', *Survival* 54/5: 113–28.

Yeisley, Mark O., 2011 'Bipolarity, Proxy Wars and the Rise of China', *Strategic Studies Quarterly* 5/4: 75–91.

Zimmermann, Doran, 2007 'Calibrating Disorder: Iran's Role in Iraq and the Coalition Response, 2003-2006', *Civil Wars*.9/1: 8–31.

Newspaper Articles

Associated Press, 2011 'China Victim of 500,000 Cyber Attacks in 2010, Says Security Agency', Guardian, 9 August 2011, available at: <http://www.guardian.co.uk/world/2011/aug/09/china-cyber-attacks>.

Becker, Jo and Scott Shane, 2012 'Secret "Kill List" Proves a Test of Obama's Principles and Will', *The New York Times*, 29 May 2012, available at: <http://www.nytimes.com/2012/05/29/world/obamas-leadership-in-war-on-al-qaeda.html?pagewanted=all>.

Bumiller, Elisabeth, 2012 'West Point is Divided on a War Doctrine's Fate', *New York Times*, 27 May 2012, available at: <http://www.nytimes.com/2012/05/28/world/at-west-point-asking-if-a-war-doctrine-was-worth-it.html?pagewanted=all>.

Ciralsky, Adam, 2010 'Tycoon, Contractor, Soldier, Spy', *Vanity Fair*, January 2010, available at: <http://www.vanityfair.com/politics/features/2010/01/blackwater-201001>.

Colvin, Marie, 2008 'Hamas Wages Iran's Proxy War on Israel', *The Sunday Times*, 9 March, available at: <http://www.thesundaytimes.co.uk/sto/news/world_news/article82296.ece>.

Fisk, Robert, 2011 'America's Secret Plan to Arm Libya's Rebels', *The Independent*, 7 March 2011, available at: <http://www.independent.co.uk/news/world/middle-east/americas-secret-plan-to-arm-libyas-rebels-2234227.html>.

Giles, Jim, 2010 'Are States Unleashing the Dogs of Cyber War?', *New Scientist* 2791, December 2010, available at: <http://www.newscientist.com/article/mg20827915.100-are-states-unleashing-the-dogs-of-cyber-war.html>.

Hopkins, Nick, 2012 'China "Targets Nato Chief" in Facebook Spying Operation', *The Observer*, 11 March 2012, available at: <http:// www.guardian.co.uk/world/2012/mar/11/china-spies-facebook-atta ck-nato>.

MacAskill, Ewan, Ian Traynor, and Robert Tait, 2007 'US Accuses Highest Levels in Iran of Supplying Deadly Weapons to Iraqi Insurgents', *Guardian*, 12 February 2007, available at: <http://www. guardian.co.uk/world/2007/feb/12/topstories3.iran>.

McDonald, Henry, 2010 'Car Bomb Explodes at Ulster Army Barracks', *Guardian*, 12 April 2010, available at: <http://www.guardian.co.uk/ uk/2010/apr/12/northern-ireland-justice-minister-david-ford>.

Natsios, Andrew S., 2012 'To Give South Sudan a Chance at Peace, Supply it with Weapons', *The Washington Post*, 13 May 2012, available at: <http://www.washingtonpost.com/opinions/to-stop-the-war-on-south-sudan-the-us-should-send-weapons/2012/05/11/gIQAywIkIU _story.html>.

Rice, Xan, Ian Traynor and Ian Black, 2011 'Libyan Rebels Loaned £800 Million in Fight to Force Gaddafi's Departure', *Guardian*, 9 June 2011, available at: <http://www.guardian.co.uk/world/2011/ jun/09/libyan-rebels-foreign-government-loans?CMP=twt_fd>.

Richburg, Keith B., 2012 'China Military Spending to Top $100 Billion in 2012, Alarming Neighbours', *The Washington Post*, 4 March 2012, available at: <http://www.washingtonpost.com/world/china-military-spending-to-top-100-billion-this-year/2012/03/04/gIQAJR nypR_story.html>.

Sanger, David, 2012 'Obama Order Sped Up Wave of Cyberattacks Against Iran', *The New York Times*, 1 June 2012, available at: <http:// www.nytimes.com/2012/06/01/world/middleeast/obama-ordered-wave-of-cyberattacks-against-iran.html?pagewanted=all>.

Tisdall, Simon, 2007 'Iran's Secret Plan for Summer Offensive to Force US out of Iraq', *Guardian*, 22 May 2007, available at: <http:// www.guardian.co.uk/world/2007/may/22/iraq.topstories3>.

Web Sources

Amnesty International Report, June 2012 *South Sudan: Overshadowed Conflict* (London), available at: <http://www.amnesty.org/en/library/ asset/AFR65/002/2012/en/67d8e84c-e990-42de-9a99-1486aab18 b1d/afr650022012en.pdf>.

BBC News online, 30 March 2011 'Obama Not Ruling Out Arming

Libya Rebels', available at: <http://www.bbc.co.uk/news/world-africa-12902450?print=true>.

BBC News online, 5 January 2012 'Obama Unveils New Strategy for 'Leaner' US Military', available at: <http://www.bbc.co.uk/news/world-us-canada-16430405?print=true>.

BBC News online, 24 February 2012 'Syria Unrest: Opposition Seeks Arms Pledge', available at: <http://www.bbc.co.uk/news/world-middle-east-17144805?print=true>.

BBC News online, 29 March 2012 'Iraq's Maliki Warns of Syria "Proxy War"', available at: <http://www.bbc.co.uk/news/world-middle-east-17544431?print=true>.

BBC News online, 30 March 2012 'UK Doubles Aid to Syrian Opposition Groups', available at: <http://www.bbc.co.uk/news/uk-17558417?print=true>.

BBC News online, 19 June 2012 'Ship "Carrying Russian Attack Helicopters to Syria" Halted off Scotland', available at: <http://www.bbc.co.uk/news/uk-scotland-highlands-islands-18503421?print=true>.

BBC News online, 25 June 2012 'MI5 Fighting "Astonishing" Level of Cyber-attacks', available at: <http://www.bbc.co.uk/news/uk-18586681?print=true>.

BBC News online, 10 August 2012 'Syria Conflict: UK to Give an Extra £5m to Opposition Groups', available at: <http://www.bbc.co.uk/news/uk-19205204?print=true>.

BBC News online, 11 October 2012 'Syrian Plane Had Illegal Cargo, says Turkey's Davutoglu', available at: <http://www.bbc.co.uk/news/world-europe-19906578?print=true>.

Center for Strategic and International Studies Report, August 2012 'Significant Cyber Incidents Since 2006', available at: <http://csis.org/files/publication/110621_Significant_Cyber_Incidents_Since_2006. pdf>.

Galster, Steve, 2001 'Afghanistan: Lessons from the Last War', Introductory Essay to the National Security Archive 'September 11th Sourcebook', available at: <www2.gwu.edu/~nsarchiv/NSAEBB/NSAEBB57/essay2.html> (note 15).

Hoffman, Frank, 2007 'Conflict in the Twenty-First Century: The Rise of Hybrid Wars' (Potomac Institute for Policy Studies), available at: <http://www.potomacinstitute.org/images/stories/publications/potomac_hybridwar_0108.pdf>.

Iraq Liberation Act, 1998 <http://www.gpo.gov/fdsys/pkg/BILLS-105hr4655enr/pdf/BILLS-105hr4655enr.pdf>.

Ivan Eland, 23 January 2002 'Turn the War on Terrorism into a War by Proxy', CATO Institute, available at: <http://www.cato.org/pub_display.php?pub_id=6660>.

Liang, Qiang, and Wang Xiansui, February 1999 'Unrestricted Warfare' (Beijing: People's Liberation Army Literature and Arts Publishing House), available at: <http://militarydispatch.com/publications/unrestrictedwarfare.pdf>.

MSNBC online, 31 January 2005 'Minister: Suicide Bomber a Handicapped Child', available at: <www.msnbc.com>.

National Security Archive 'September 11th Sourcebook', available at: <www2.gwu.edu/~nsarchiv/NSAEBB/NSAEBB57/essay2.html>.

Transcript from evidence of Tony Blair at Chilcot Iraq Inquiry, 29 January 2010, available at: <http://www.iraqinquiry.org.uk/media/43909/100129-blair.pdf>.

Webcast of US Defense Secretary Leon Panetta's testimony before Senate Armed Services Committee, March 2012, available at: <http://senate.gov/fplayers/jw57/urlMP4Player.cfm?fn=armed037&st=1120&dur=9960>.

Index